THE ISLAND OF SARK may be small but it is something very special.

Life is quieter here as no cars are allowed, the only means of transport are bicycles, horsedrawn carriages and working tractors.

Although it is only 3 miles long by 1.5 miles wide Sark has a long coastline of particular beauty and full of surprises. There are many interesting caves, outcrops and gullies as well as open sandy bays.

The different seasons add their varying colours to the cliff tops, roadside verges and fields.

There is always something new to discover no matter how often one visits Sark.

ABOVE: No. 2 May is the month for foxgloves and the island can certainly put on a fine display. This view was taken in Little Sark near Port Gorey. Guernsey can be seen in the background.

LEFT: No. 3 Point Robert lighthouse greets sea travellers on the approach to Maseline Harbour. The lighthouse was built in 1912 from Eperquerie stone and is now operated automatically.

BOTTOM: No. 4 Visiting boats anchor in Maseline Bay sheltered by the east coast cliffs.

OPPOSITE TOP: No. 5 The passenger ferry, Le Bon Marin de Serk, approaches Sark's principal harbour at La Maseline. Construction was started on the harbour in 1938 but was interrupted by the war. It was eventually completed in 1947 and formally opened by the Duke of Edinburgh in June 1949.

OPPOSITE BOTTOM: No. 6 A tractor is carefully reversed onto the busy jetty at La Maseline. The driver has come to collect luggage for the island hotels.

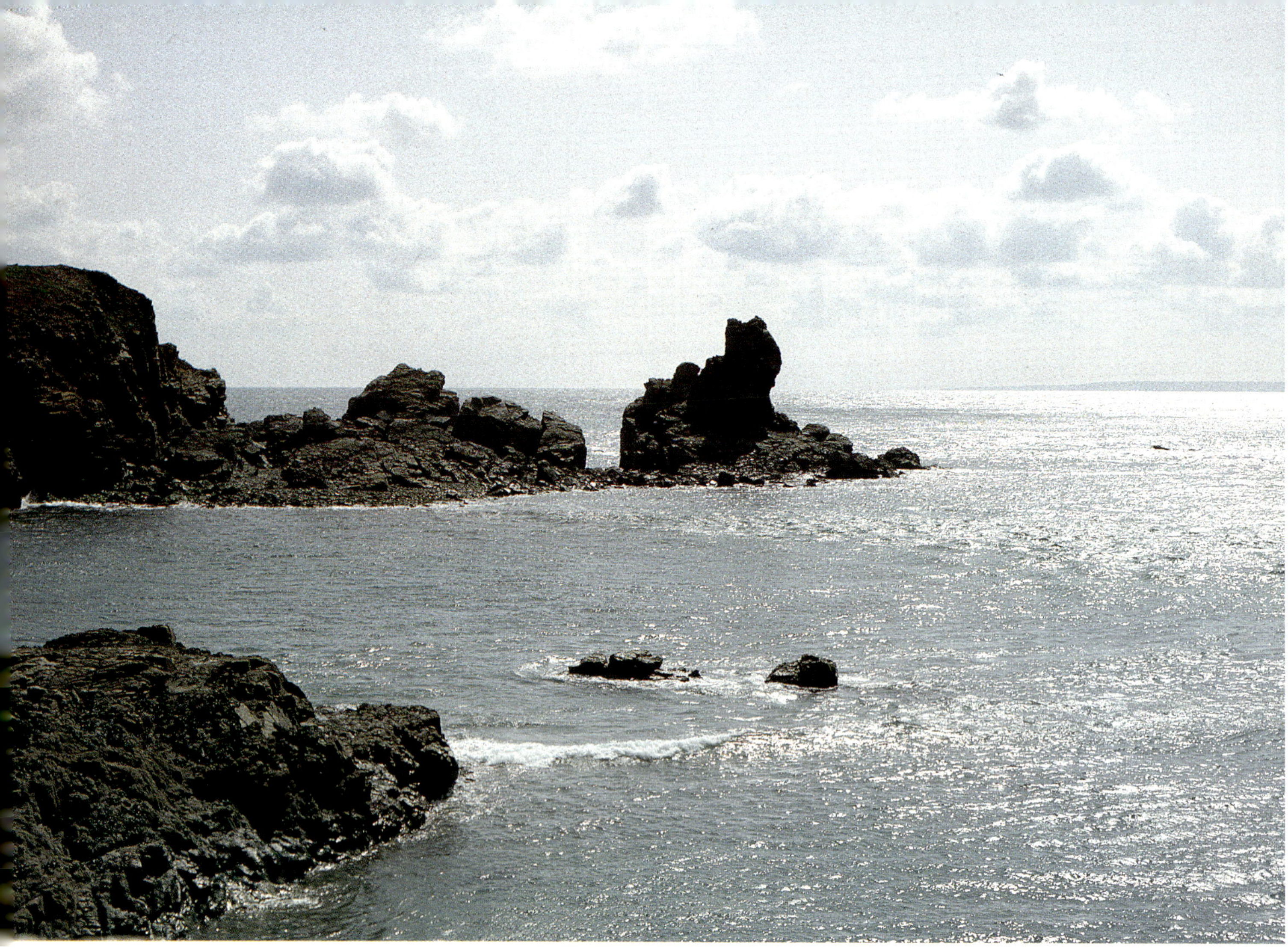

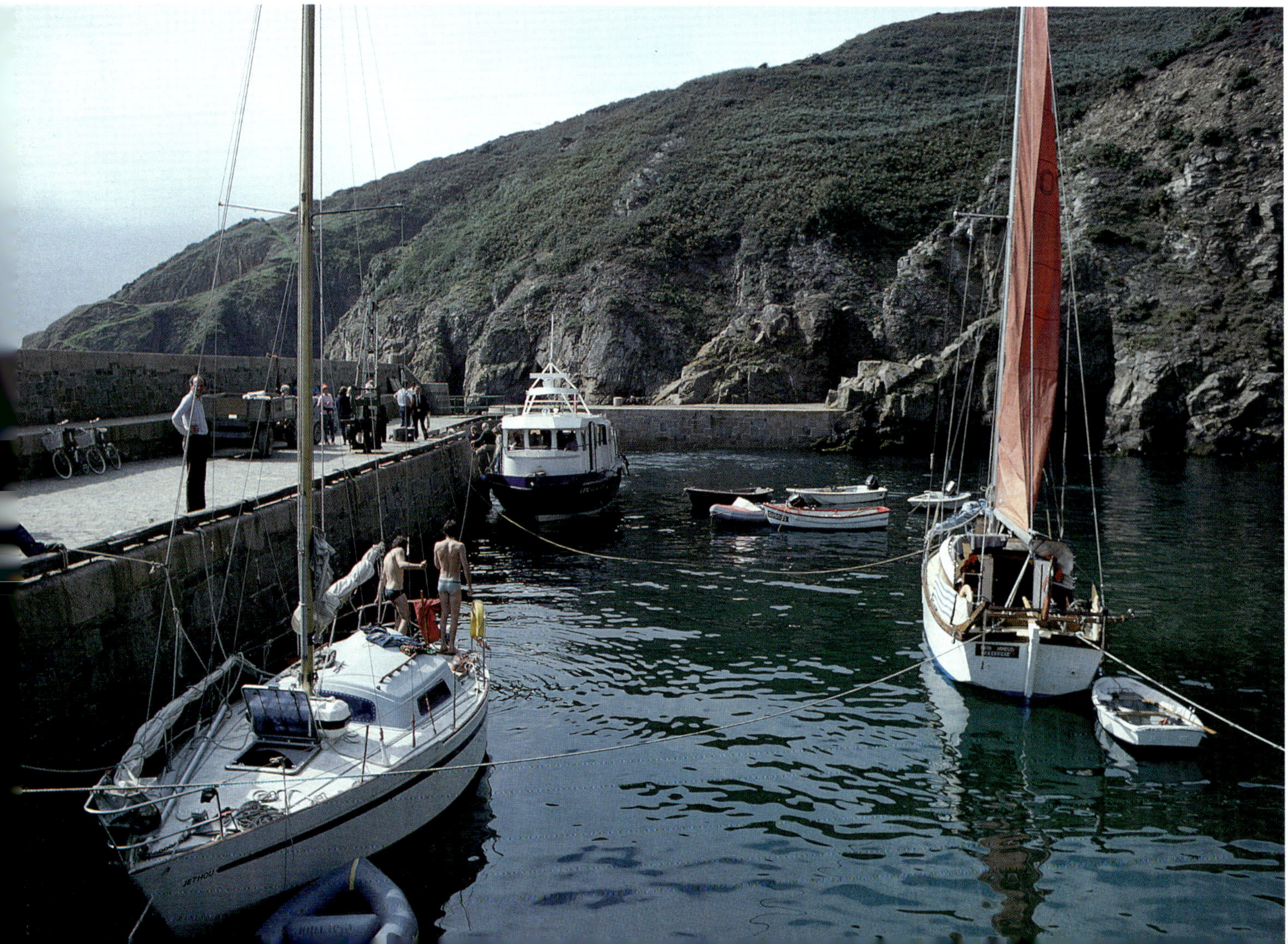

OPPOSITE TOP: No. 7 The rugged outlines of Les Bûrons Islets, which includes the distinctive Cat Rock, lie just off the Creux Harbour.

OPPOSITE BOTTOM: No. 8 Small but beautiful, Le Creux Harbour. Created in La Baie de la Motte in the 1570's by Helier de Carteret, the first Seigneur of Sark. The breakwater arms were later additions and not completed until the late 1800's.

TOP: No. 9 Looking down on Creux Harbour from the cliff path that leads to Les Lâches anchorage. The stretch of water between the harbour and Les Bûrons Islets is called Le Gulet (the Gullet).

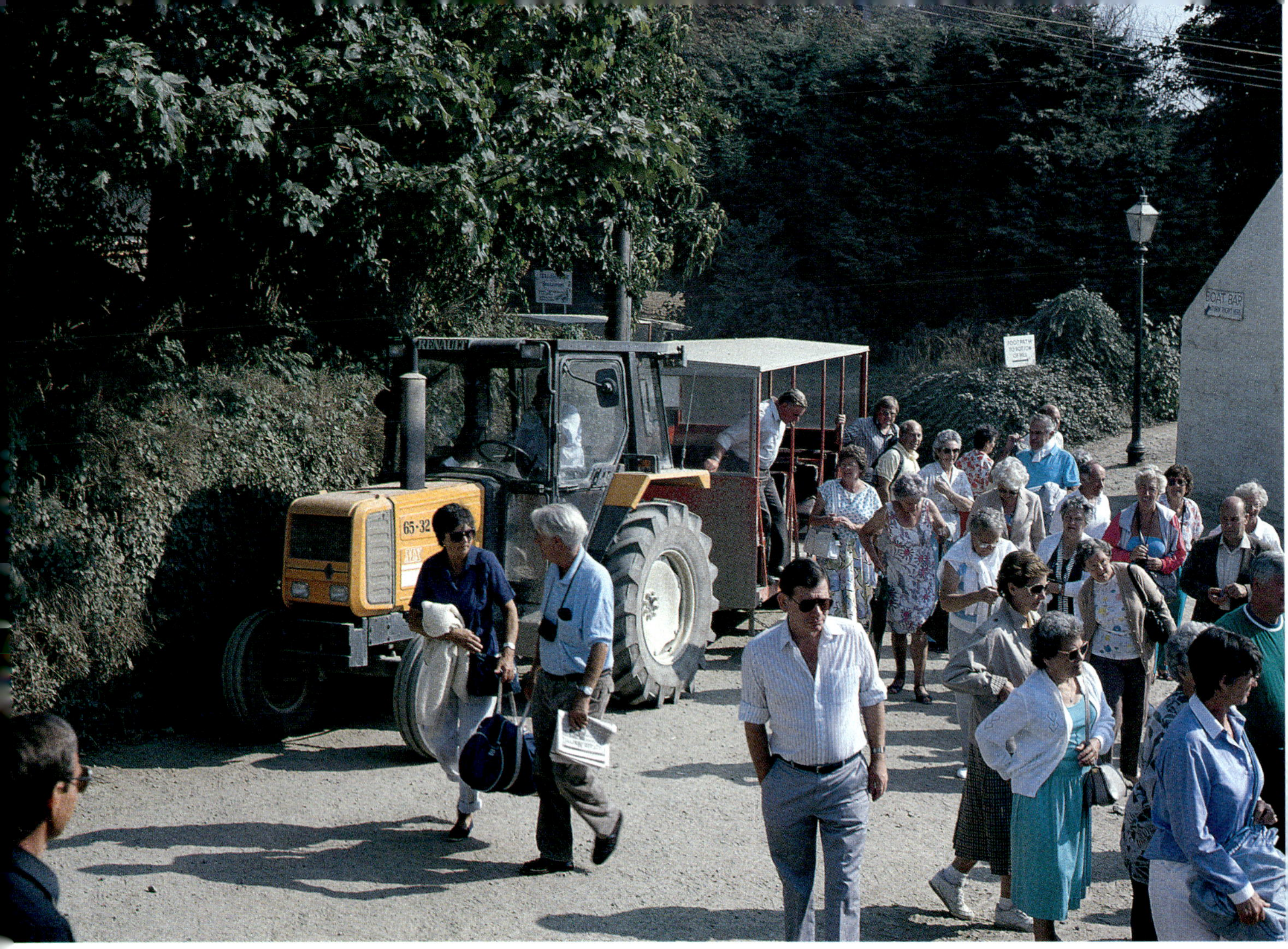

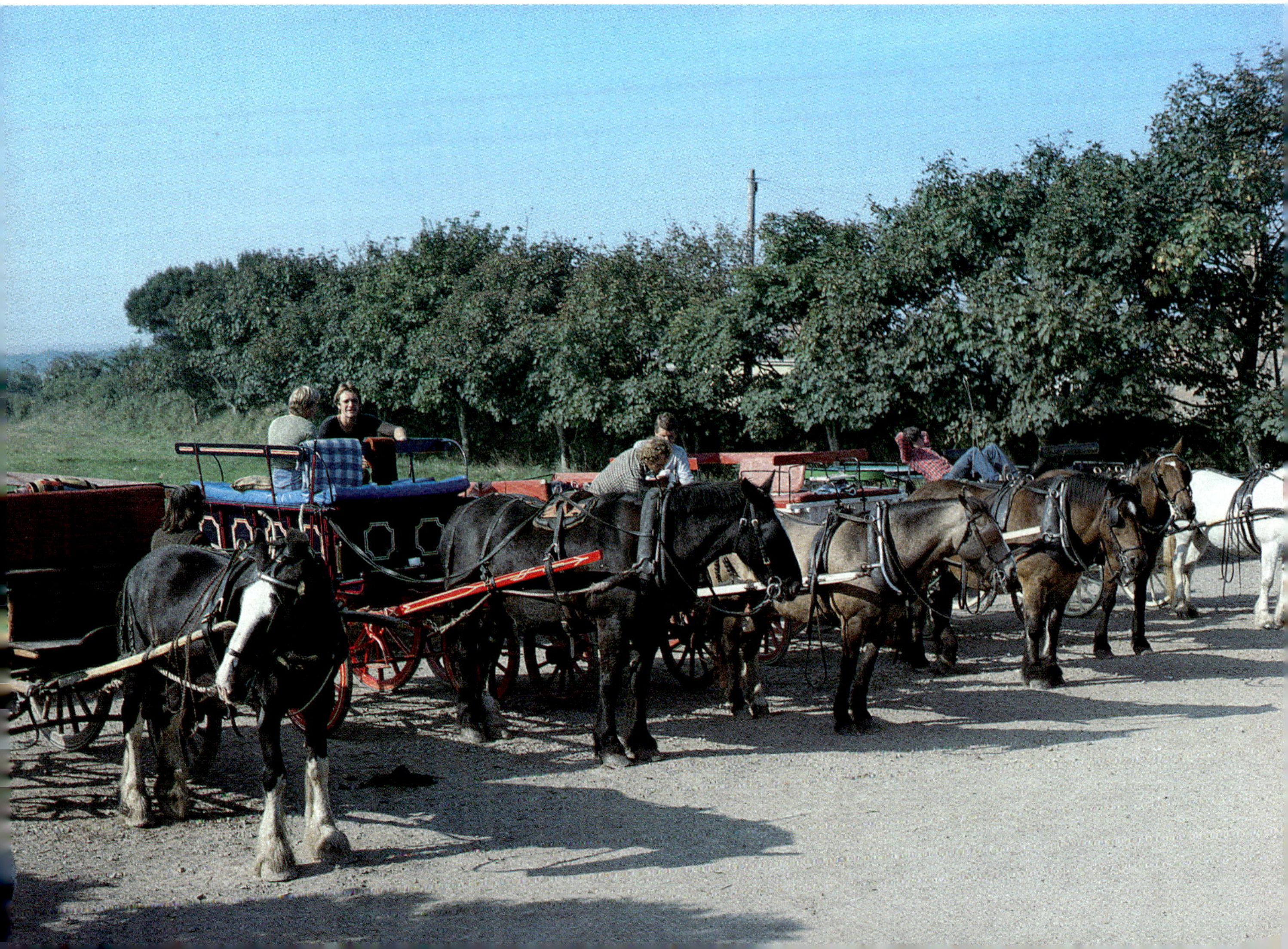

OPPOSITE TOP: No. 10 The easiest way to tackle the Harbour Hill is by a tractor-drawn trailer, affectionately nicknamed the "Toast-rack". Here it is seen with its passengers at the Bel Air Tavern.

OPPOSITE BOTTOM: No. 11 Horses and carriages lined up at the top of the harbour hill waiting to take tourists for a trip around the island.

TOP: No. 12 No work today for these horses being led along Rue Lucas from the crossroads at La Collinette.

RIGHT: No. 13 Johnnie with his horse Rosie.

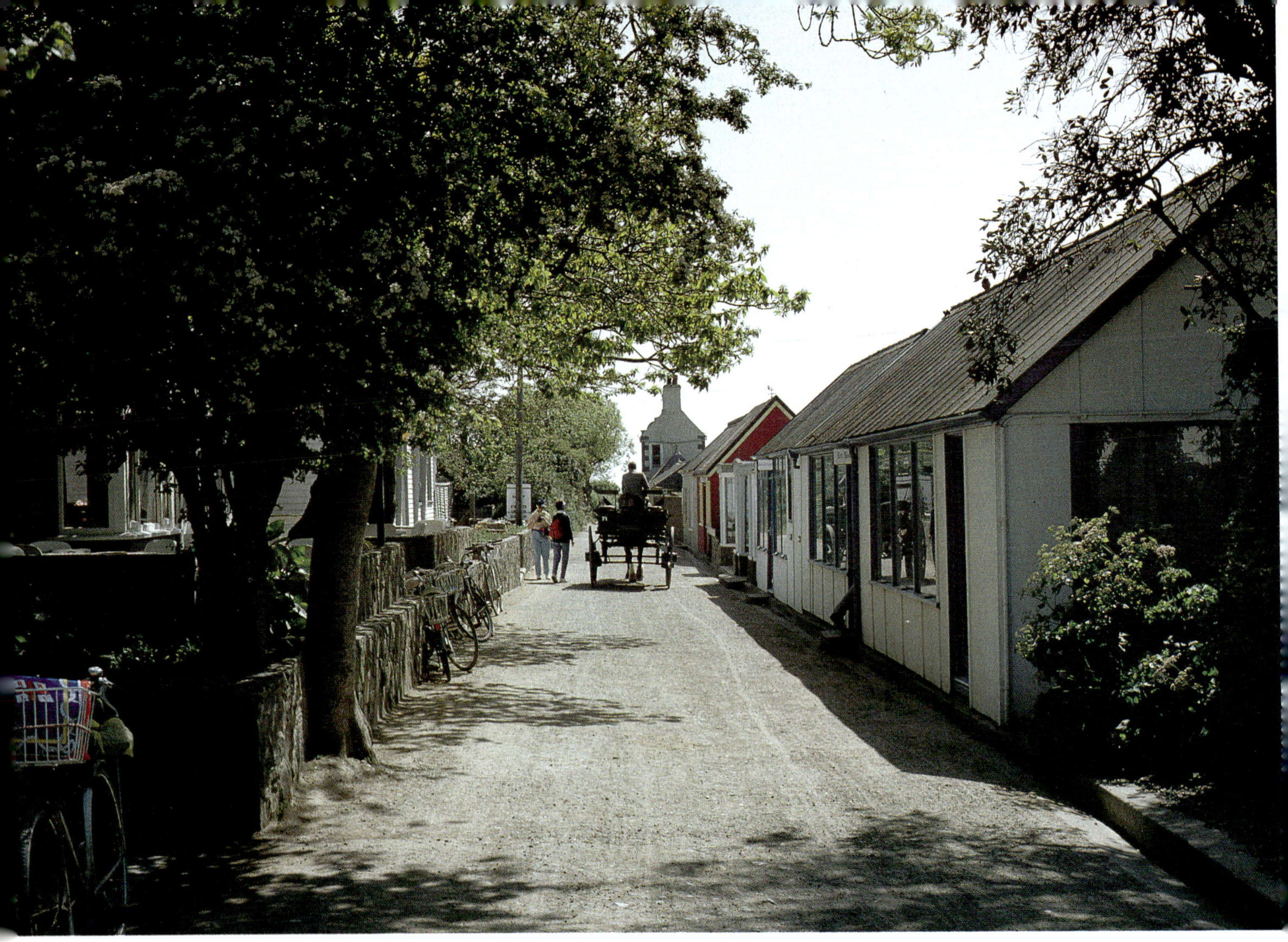

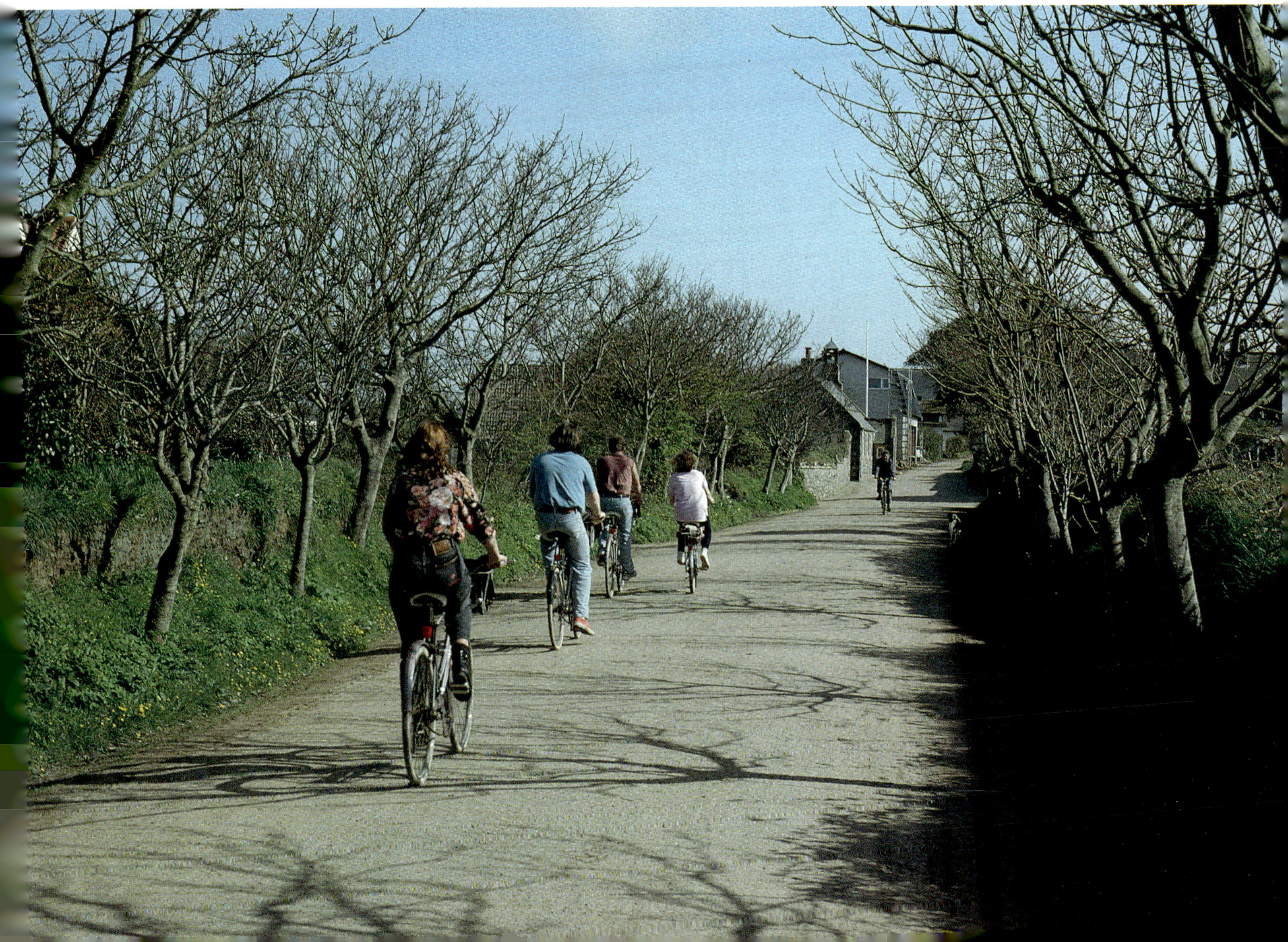

OPPOSITE TOP: No. 14 The Avenue, once lined with trees, is Sark's main shopping centre with a variety of shops of different shapes and sizes.

OPPOSITE BOTTOM: No. 15 Cycling is a popular way to get around Sark especially on a day trip. These cyclists on Rue la Rade are approaching the crossroads near the school.

RIGHT: No. 16 You need a good head for heights if you are investigating the moorings at Les Lâches, as this chasm is just to the right of the track.

BOTTOM: No. 17 A view of Derrible Point from the top of the cliff path. Taken in the Spring this shows the wealth of flowers which border the tracks around the island's coastline.

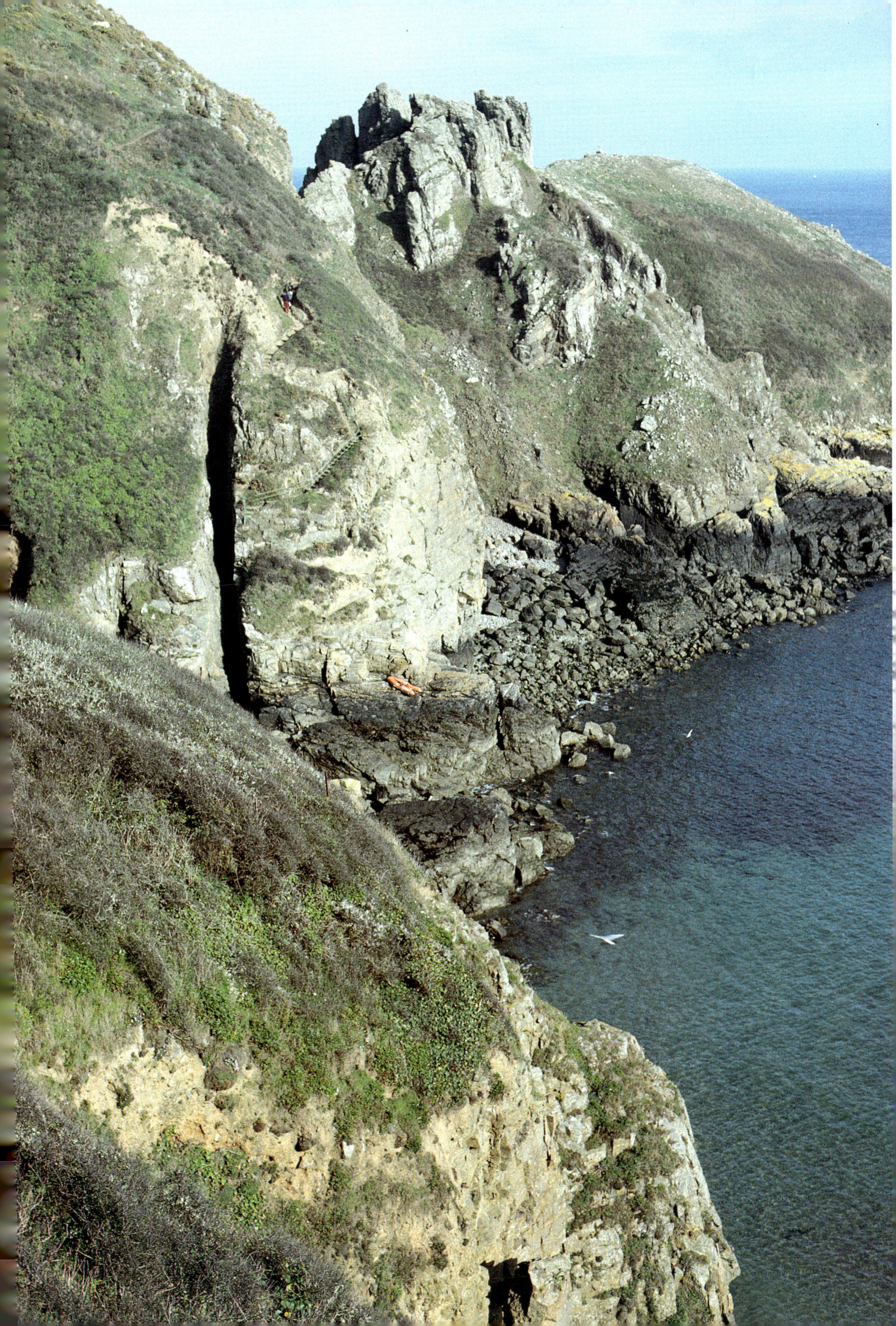

Derrible Bay. OPPOSITE: No. 18 The east side of the bay with the path winding down until it reaches a rocky platform. This is a good place to sit while waiting for the tide to drop and allow access to the bay.

TOP LEFT: No. 19 The view to the West with a visiting French yacht at anchor.

TOP RIGHT: No. 20 Creux Derrible, a large cave with its roof fallen in. At low tide there is access to the cave through two tunnels in the base of the cliff face.

RIGHT: No. 21 This face in the rock is on a large outcrop rising from the beach.

TOP: No. 22 A cow grazes near the track that leads from La Peigneurie down into Dixcart Valley and the bay. The conical rock out to sea is L'Etac which is situated at the southern end of Little Sark.

LEFT: No.23 A view from the Hogs Back showing Petit Dixcart surrounded by the trees in Dixcart Valley.

OPPOSITE TOP: No. 24 A fork in the path with the left route carrying on down to Dixcart Bay and the right leading upward to the top of the cliff.

OPPOSITE BOTTOM: No. 25 An old Napoleonic cannon lies half buried in the ground on top of the Hogs Back. This is one of nine which were positioned on various headlands to repulse invaders.

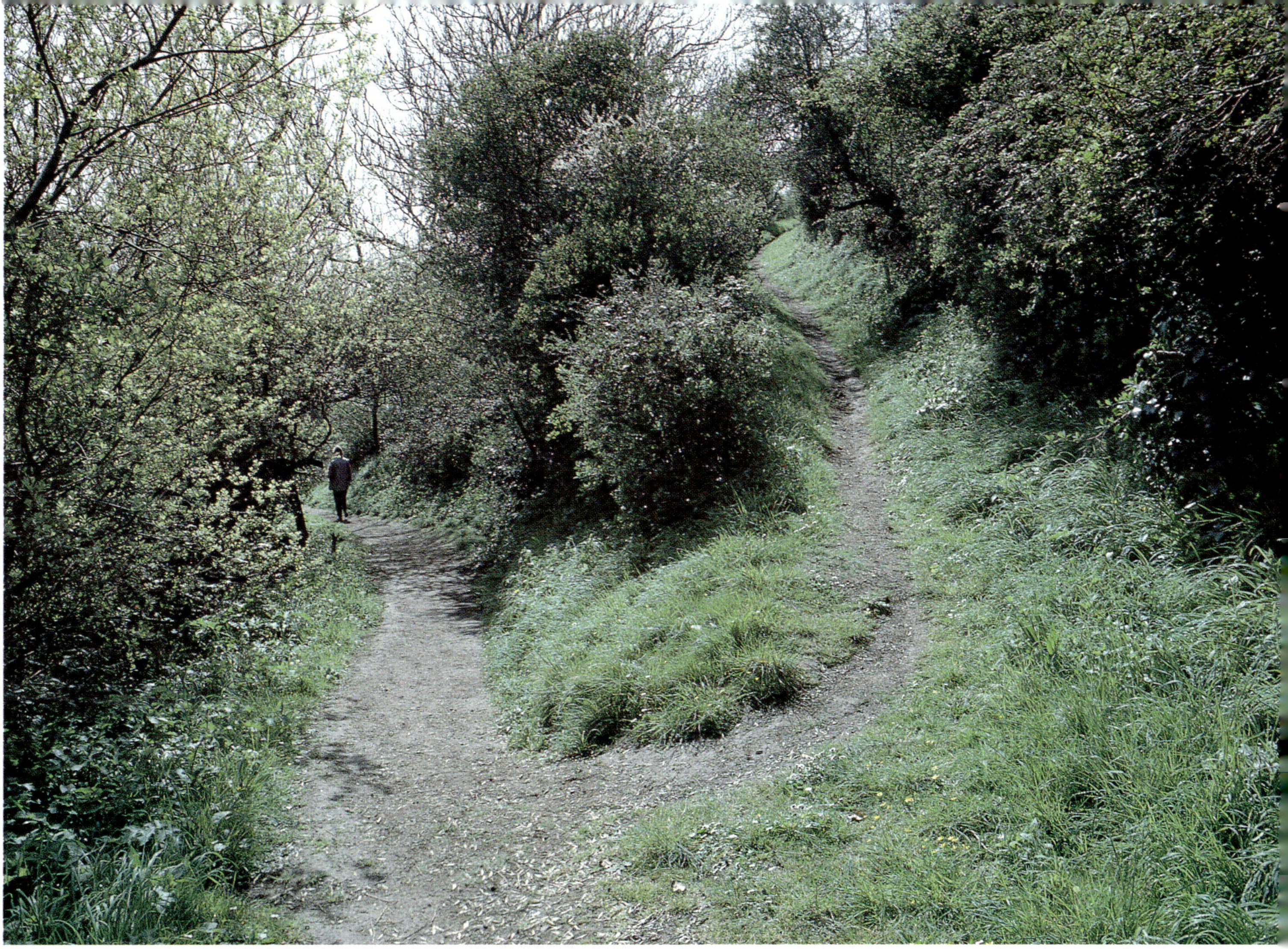

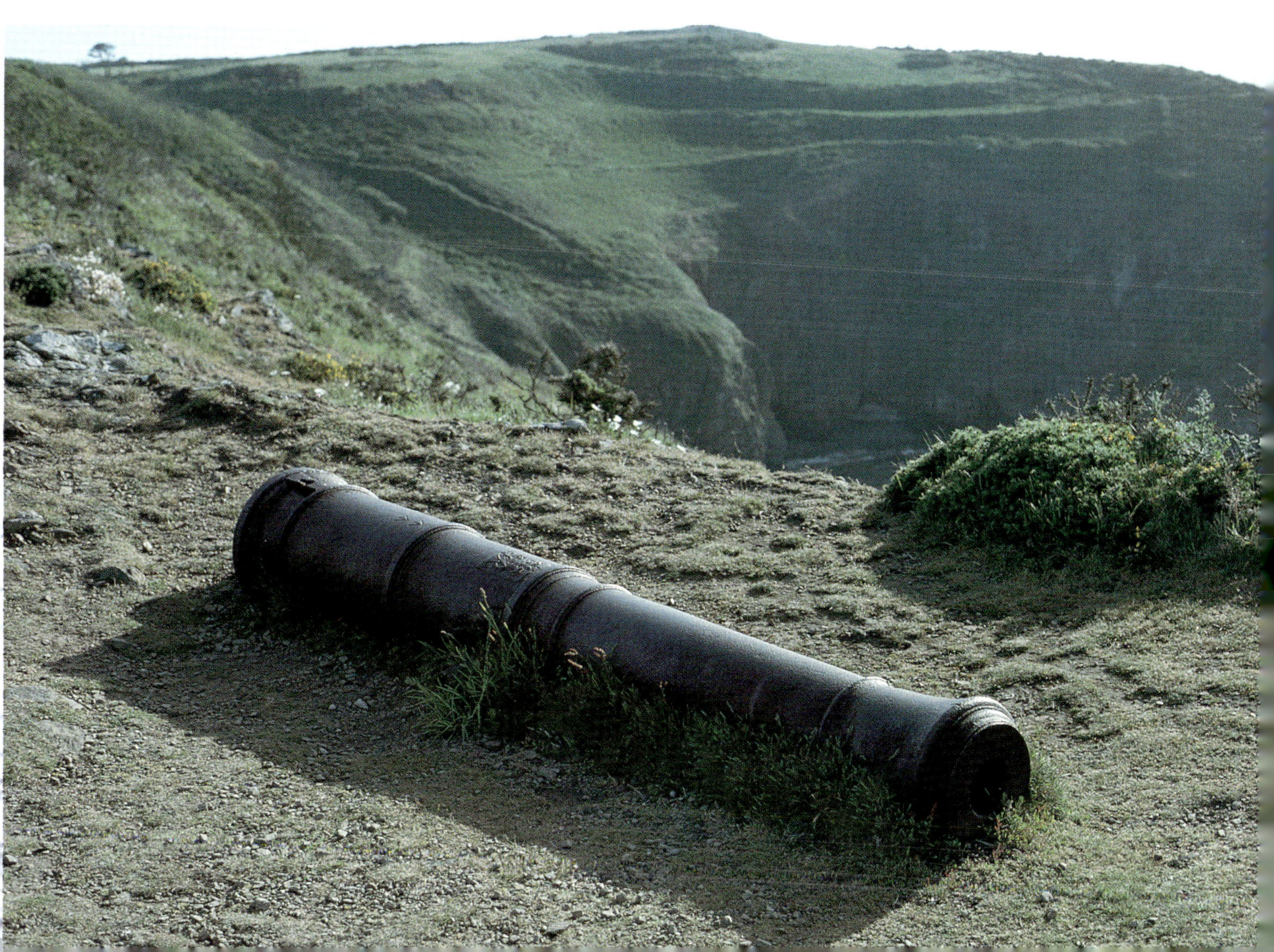

Dixcart Bay. No. 26 Looking down into the bay from the Hogs Back. There is good anchorage here for visiting boats especially when the wind is in the west.

OPPOSITE TOP: No. 27 Easy to reach and the most popular bay in Sark. At low tide there is a large expanse of sand to enjoy and an interesting rock coastline to explore.

OPPOSITE BOTTOM: No. 28 Having fun at the water's edge.

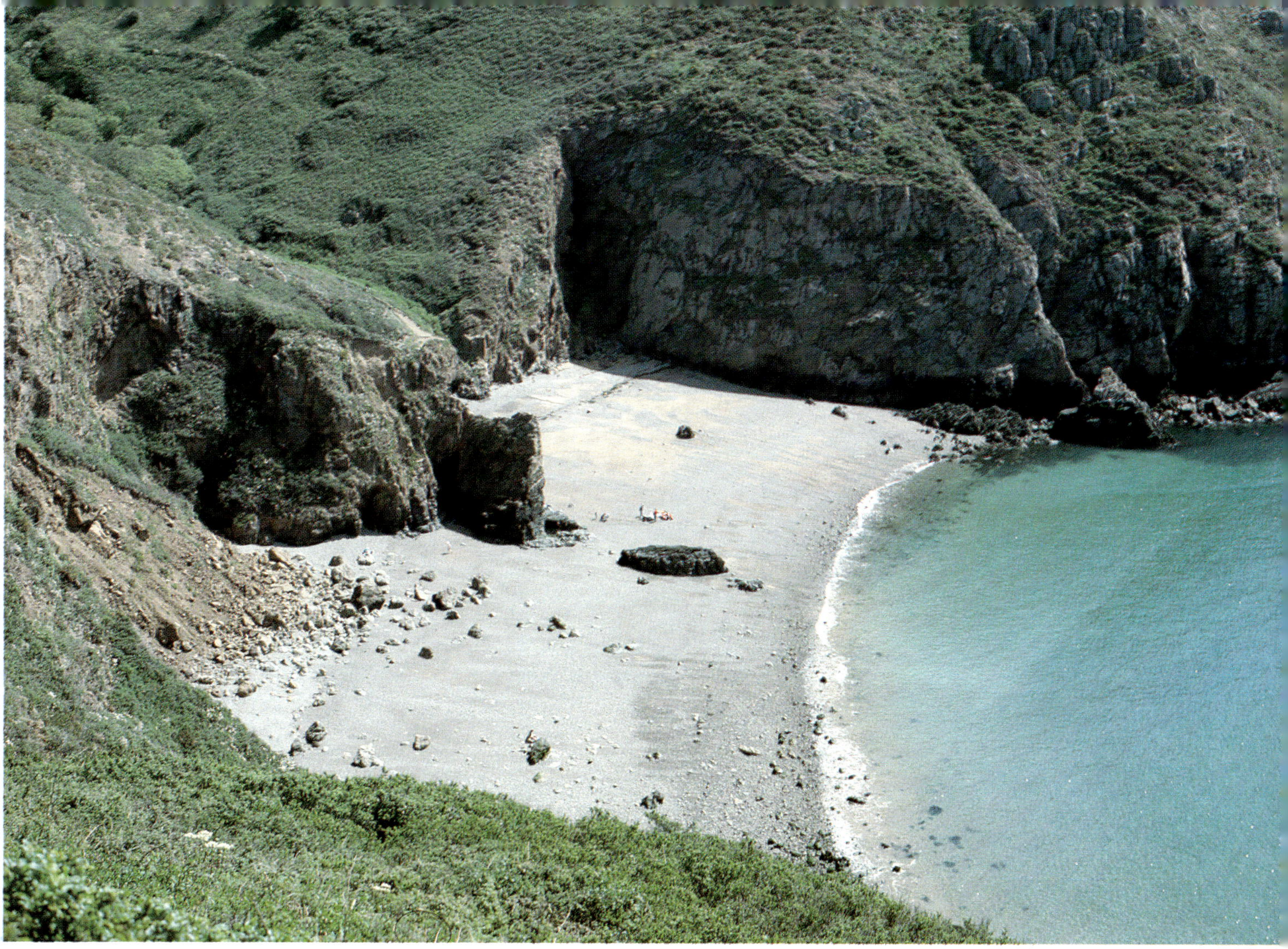

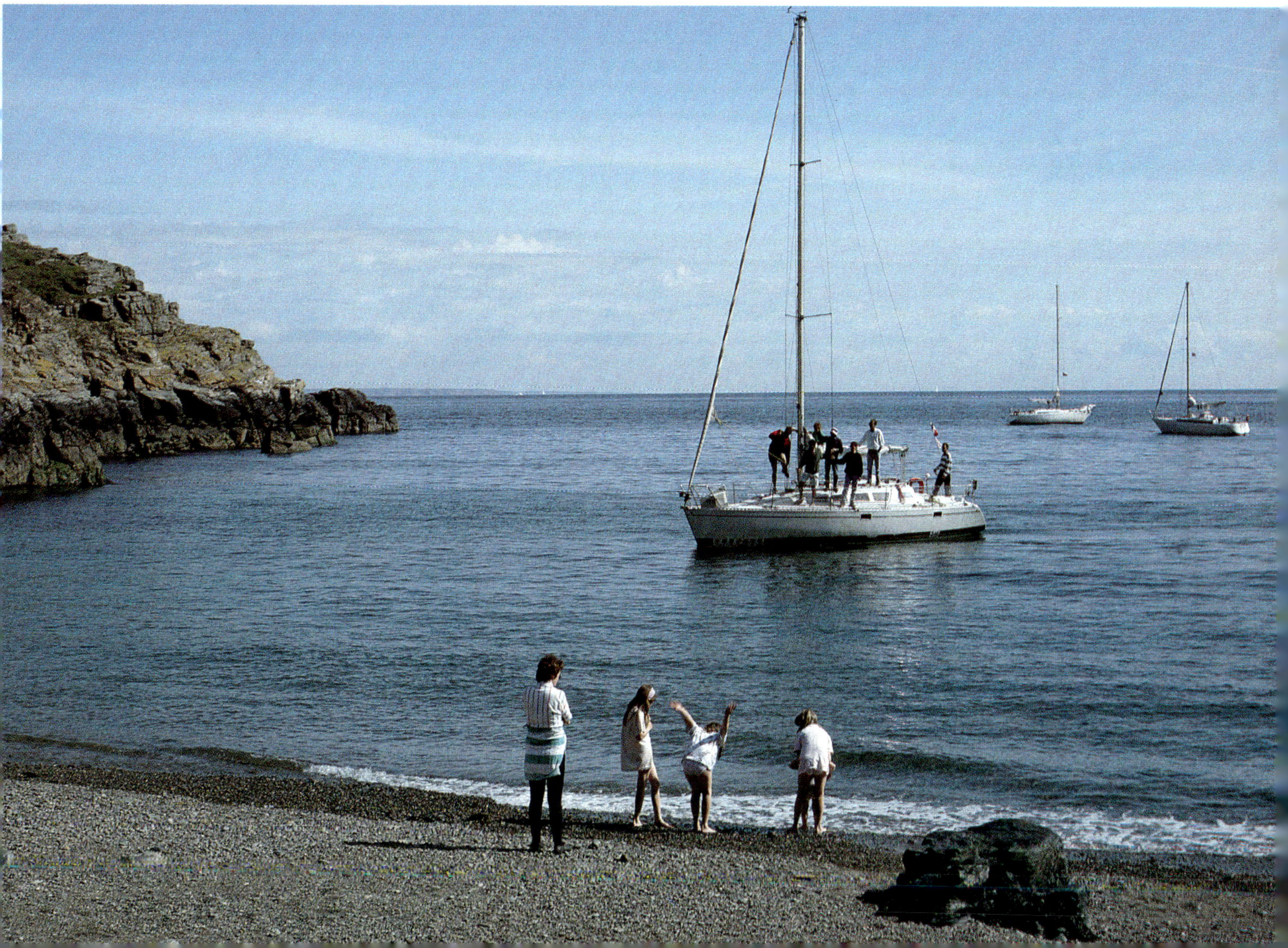

TOP: No. 29 A carriage passes Le Manoir on Rue de Moulin. This was the home of the Seigneurs of the Island up to the year 1730 and then it was a parsonage for 200 years.

LEFT: No. 30 This thick walled cottage is the oldest part of Le Manoir and was the home of Helier de Carteret, the first Seigneur of Sark.

OPPOSITE TOP: No. 31 A path opposite Le Manoir leads down into Dixcart Valley and Stocks Hotel, a popular place to stay and renowned for its lobster lunches.

OPPOSITE BOTTOM: No. 32 A little further down the valley is Dixcart Hotel another of Sark's fine Hotels.

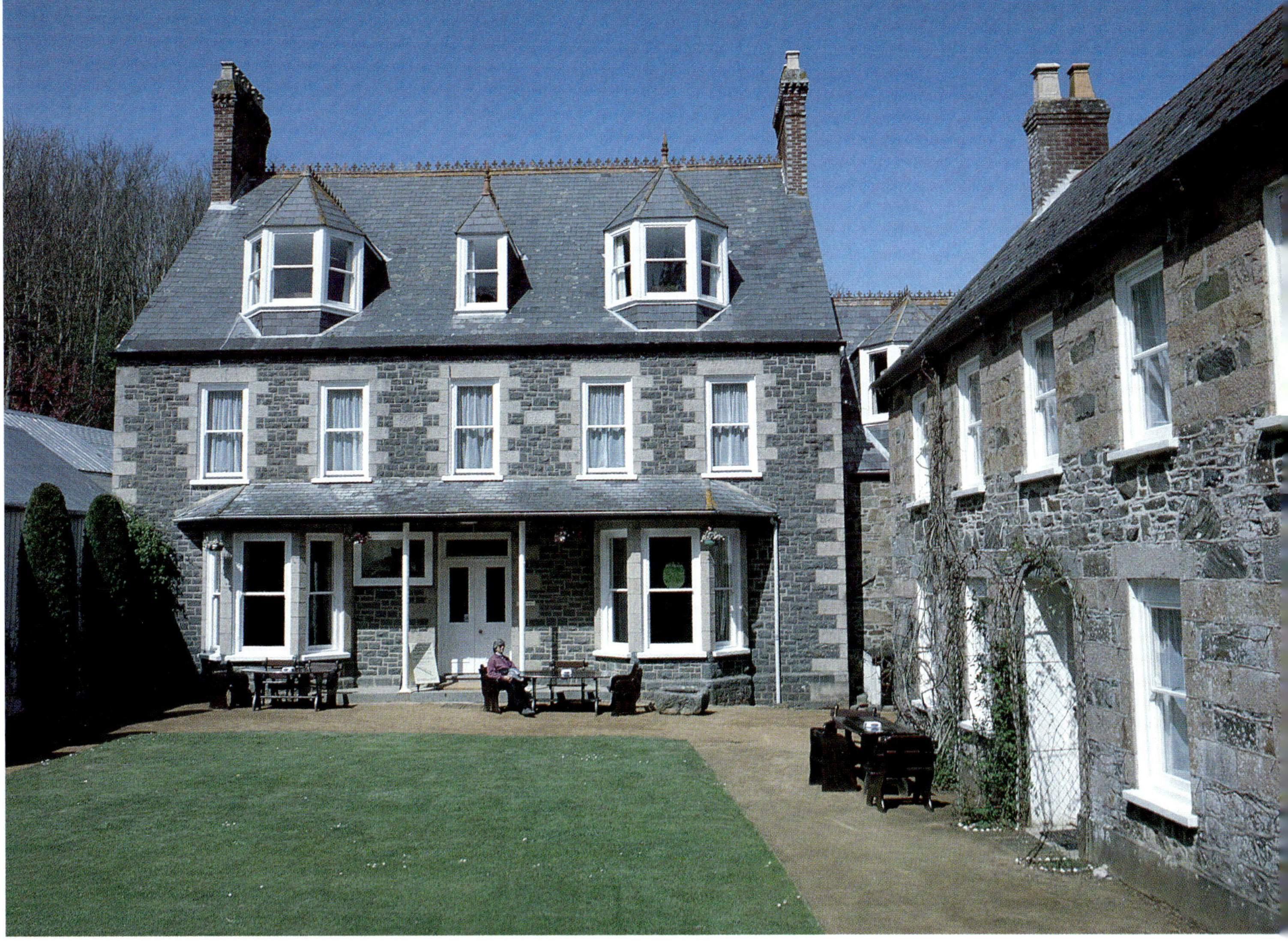

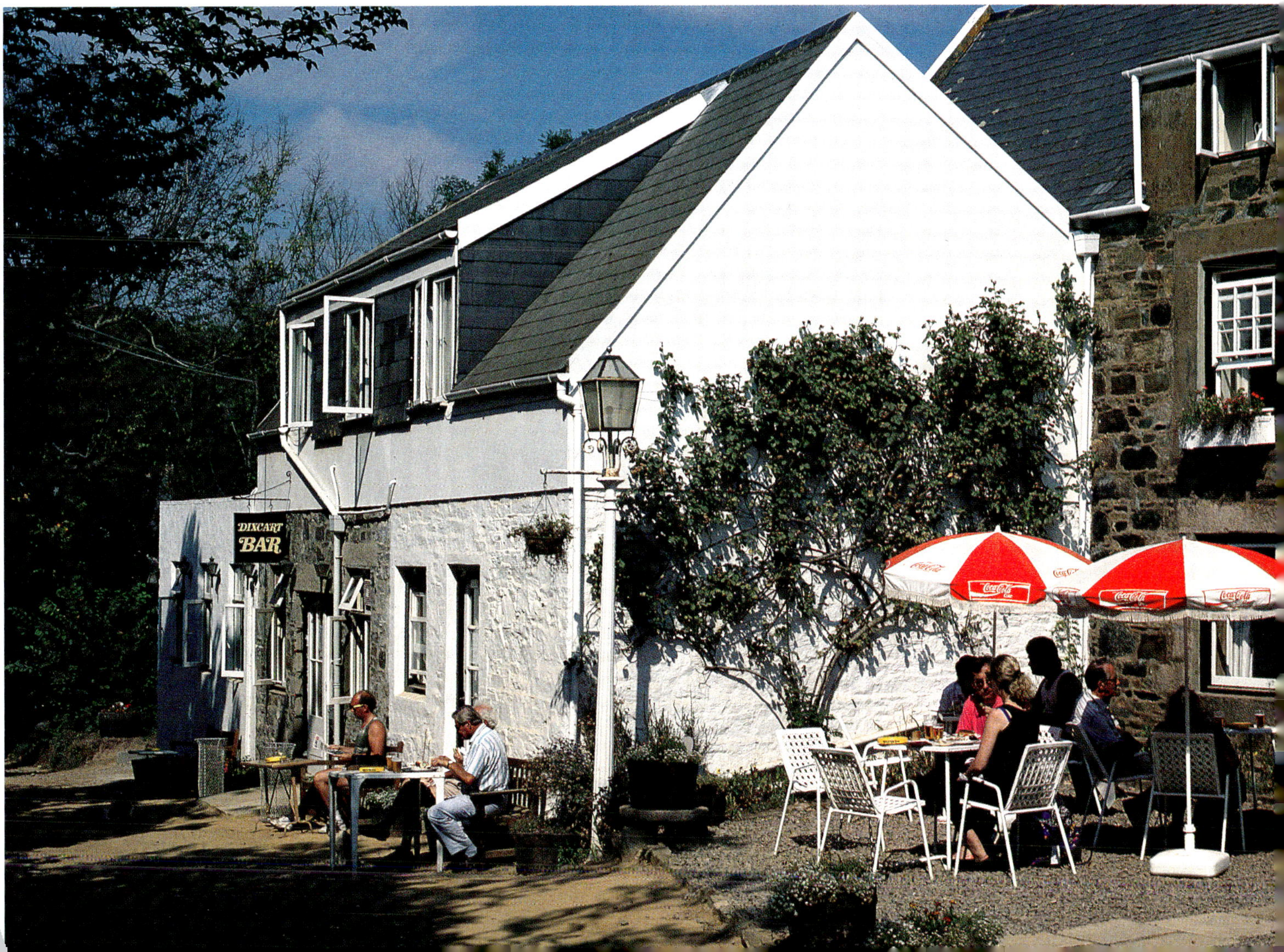
DIXCART
BAR

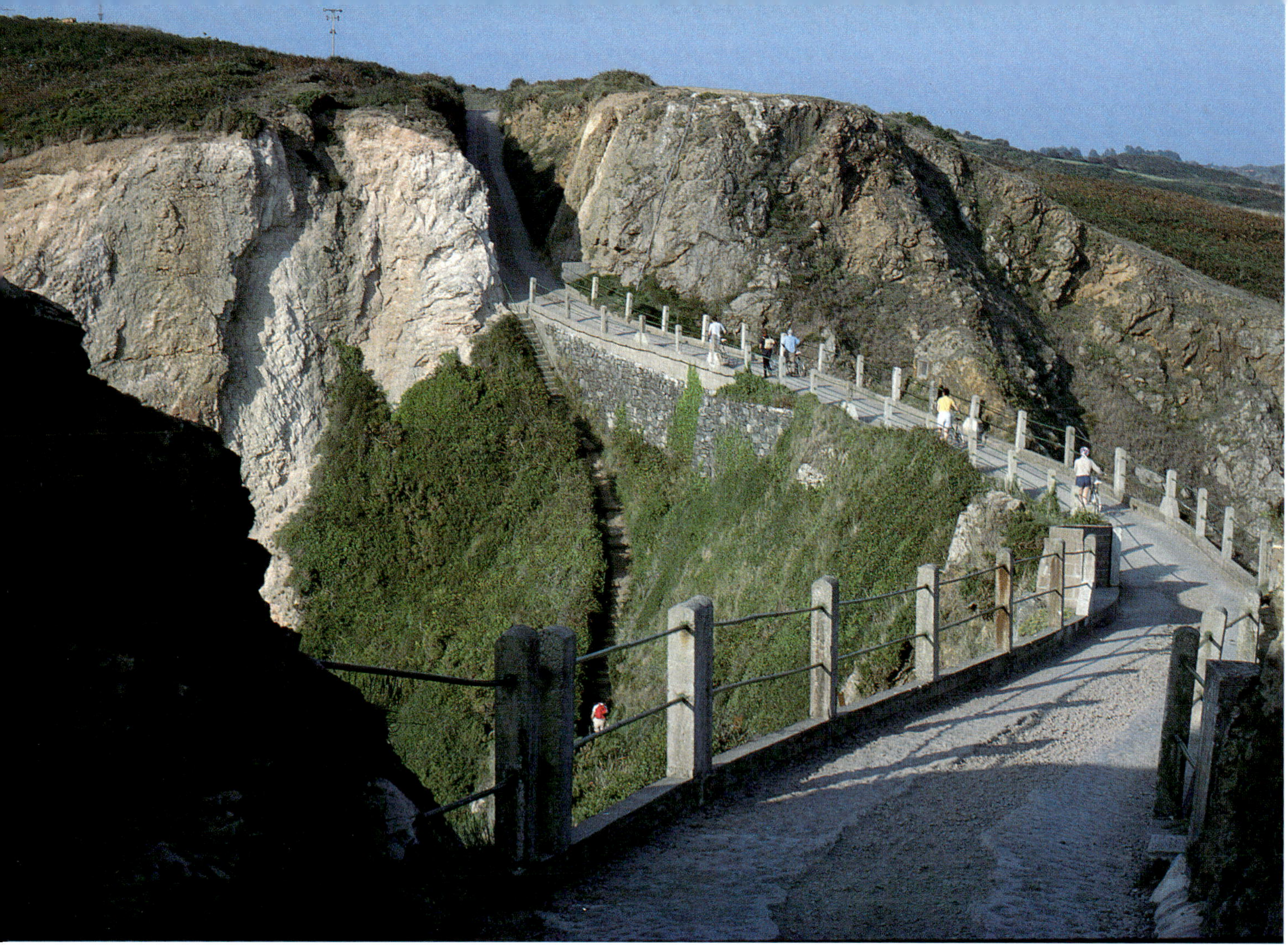

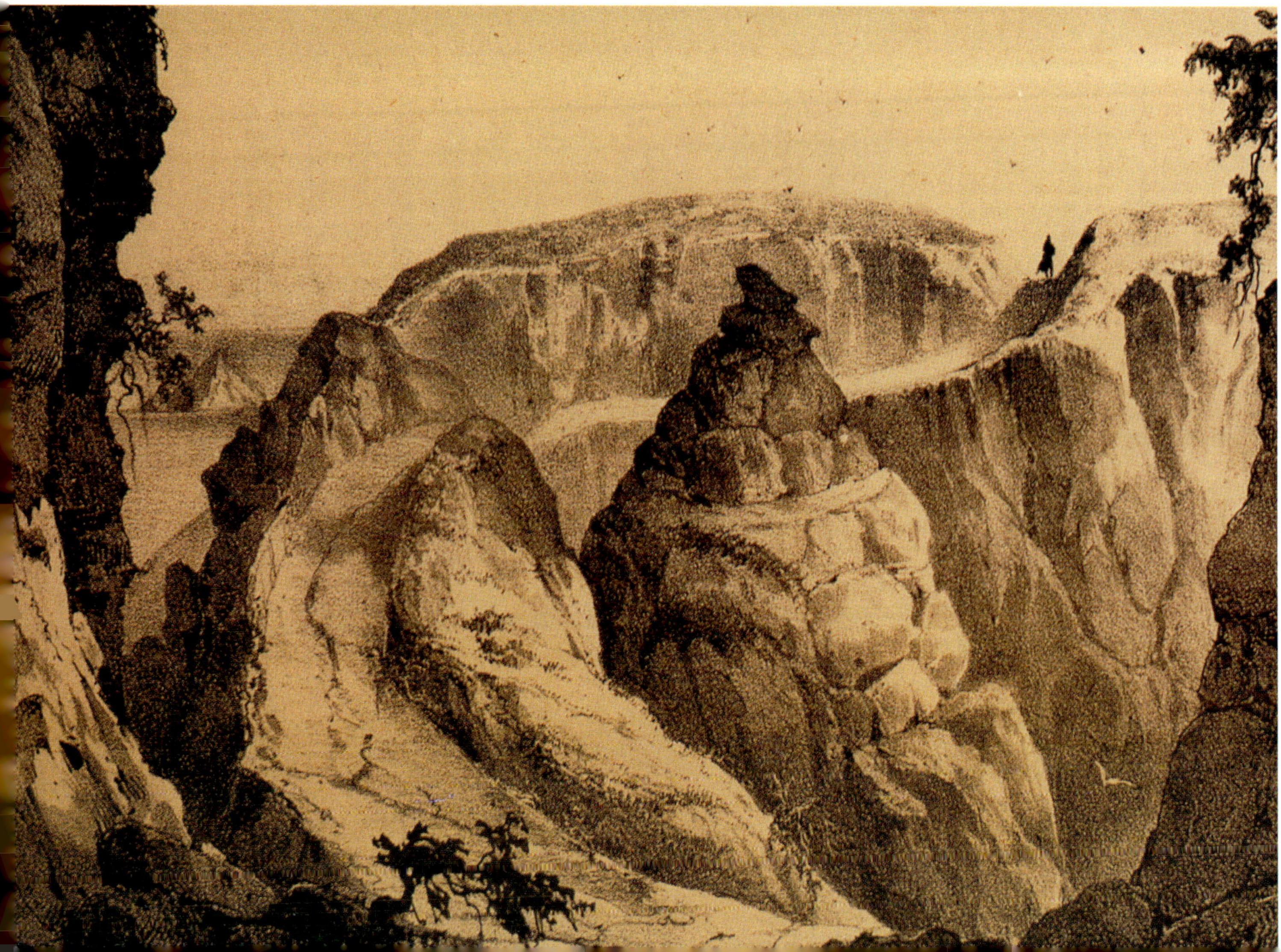

OPPOSITE TOP: No. 33 La Coupée. The narrow causeway joining the two Islands as viewed from Little Sark. A narrow pathway can be seen leading down the cliff to Grande Grève Bay.

OPPOSITE BOTTOM: No. 34 An old lithoprint from the early 1800's looking from Big Sark towards Little Sark. In those days crossing the Coupée needed care and was especially hazardous in strong winds.

ABOVE: No. 35 A tight squeeze as a horse and carriage is led across La Coupée. The bay in the background is Grande Grève.

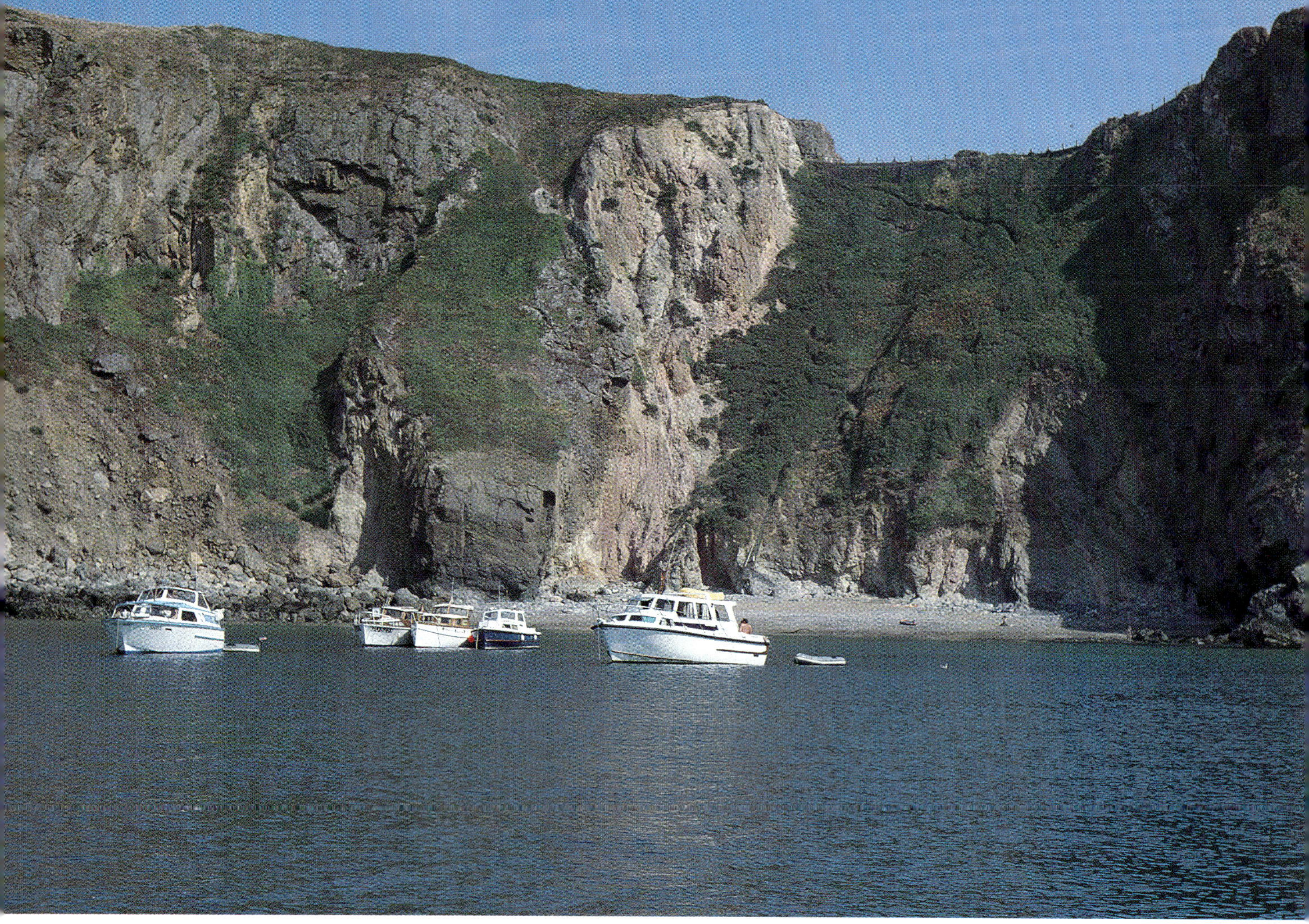

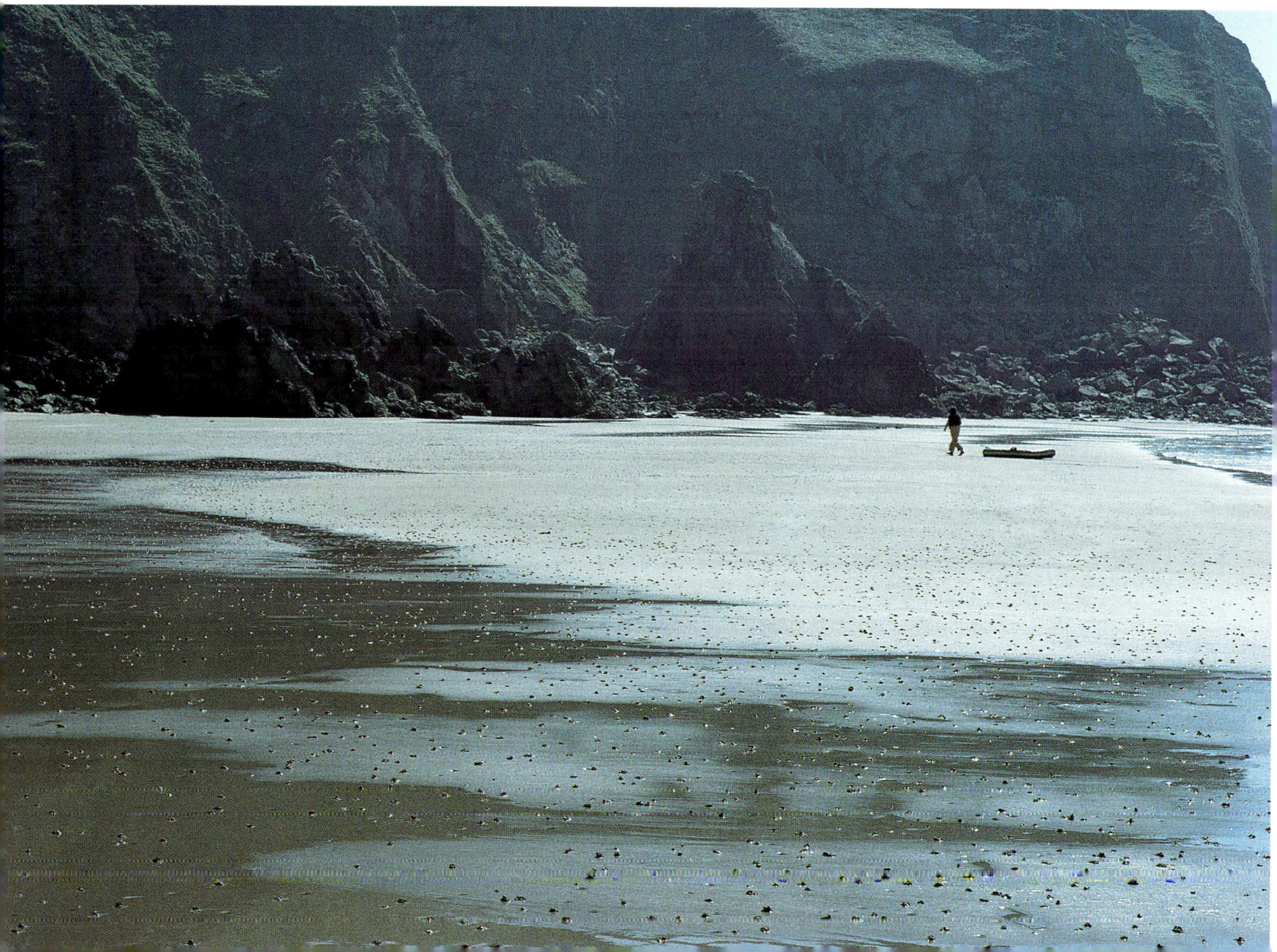

Grande Grève. OPPOSITE TOP: No. 36 The bay as seen from the sea. This is a popular haven for small craft when the wind is in the east.

OPPOSITE BOTTOM: No. 37 A wide expanse of inviting sand is revealed at low tide.

ABOVE: No. 38 Looking down on the cliffs that border the north side of the bay. In the background is the Island of Brecqhou.

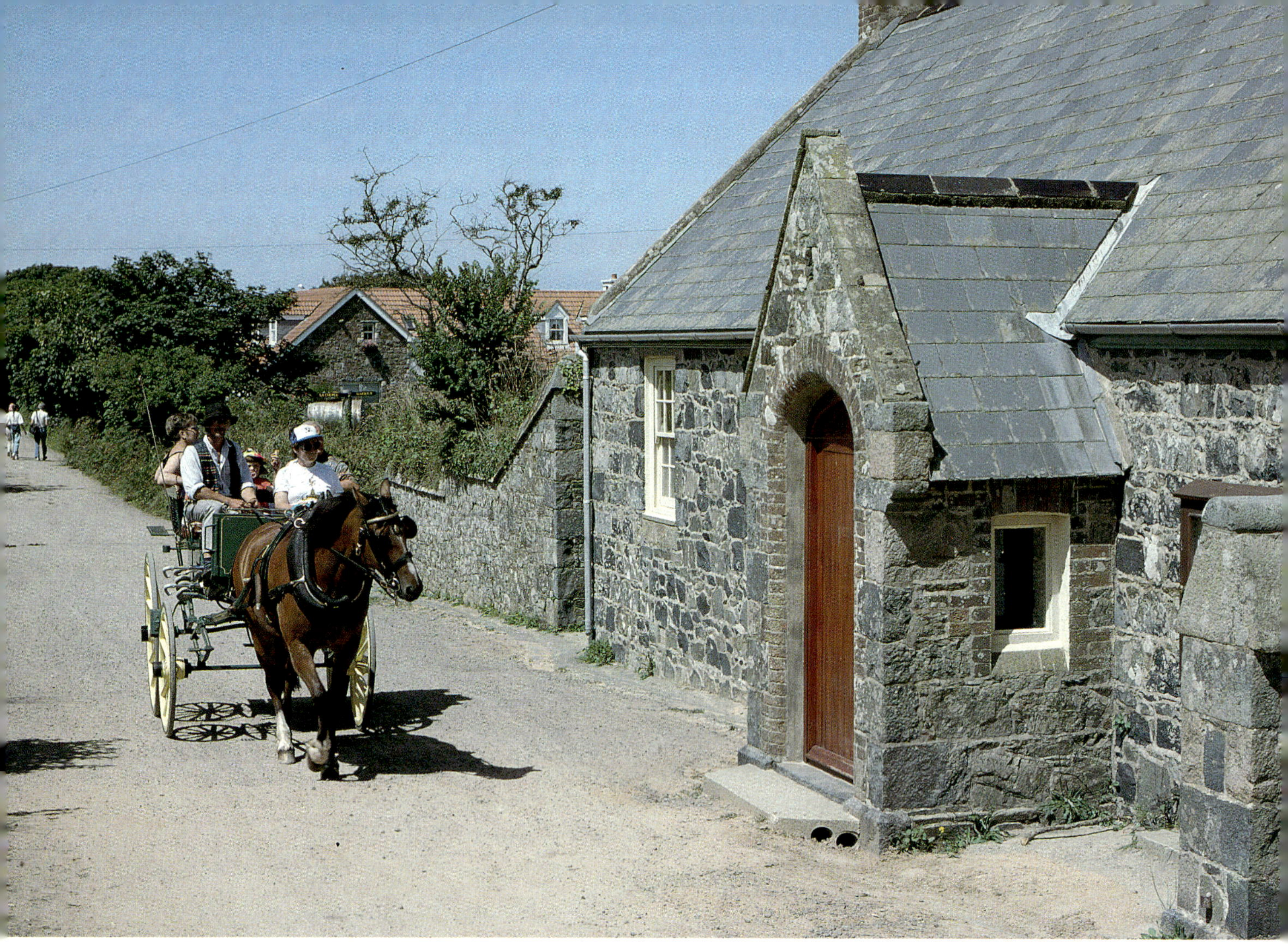

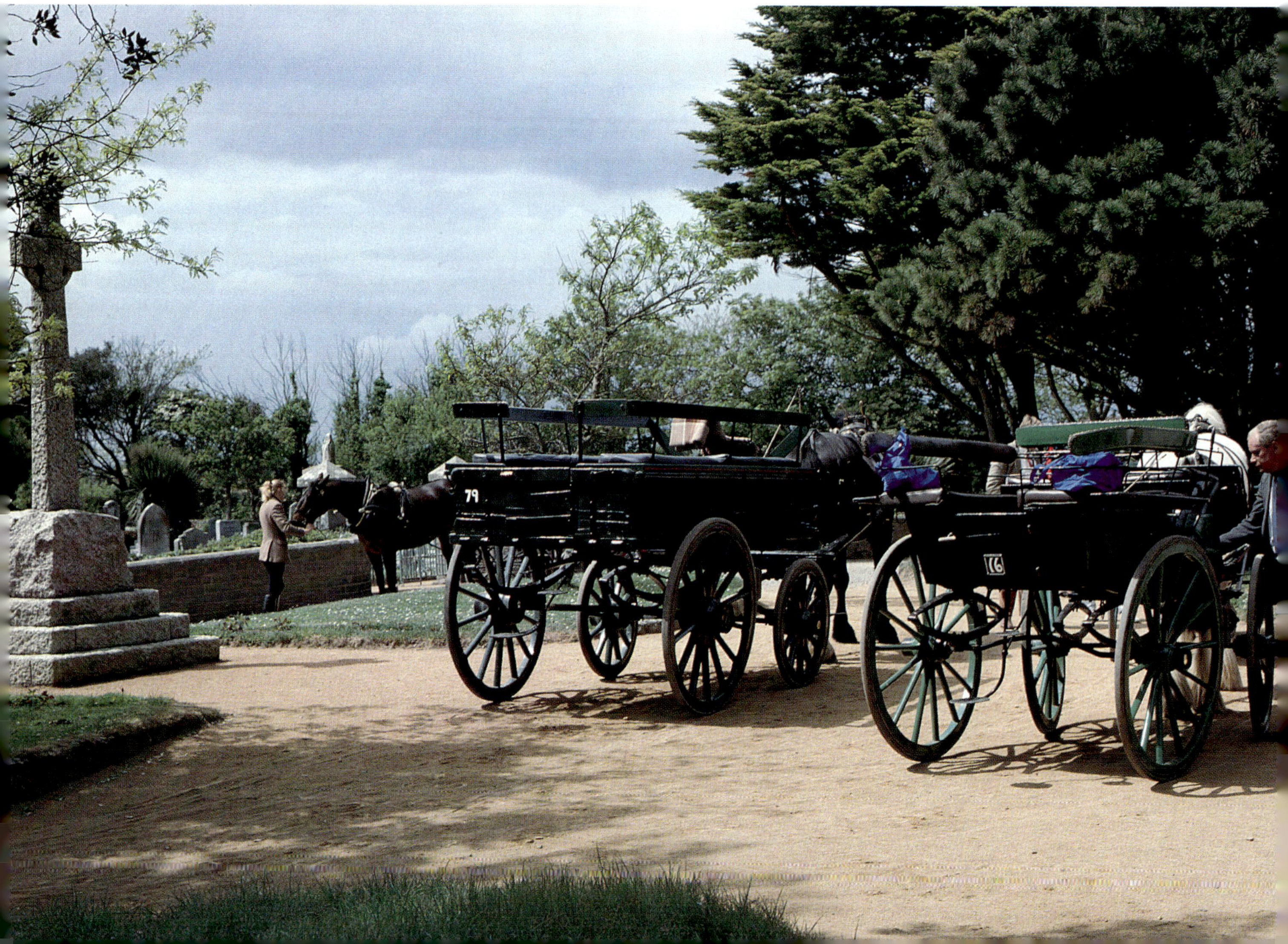
79
16

OPPOSITE TOP: No. 39 A carriage passes the Senior School which was built in the 1820's through the campaigning of Pierre Le Pelley, the Seigneur at that time. This is also the meeting place of the Sark Government, known as the Chief Pleas.

OPPOSITE BOTTOM: No. 40 Taking a break outside St. Peter's Church.

TOP LEFT: No. 41 This unusual gateway on the corner of a field near the Seigneurie was originally part of an old Guernsey farmhouse. The field beyond the gate is where the annual Horse Show is held.

TOP RIGHT: No. 42 Taking it easy at the show.

ABOVE: No. 43 Spectators and competitors enjoying a sunny day at the Show.

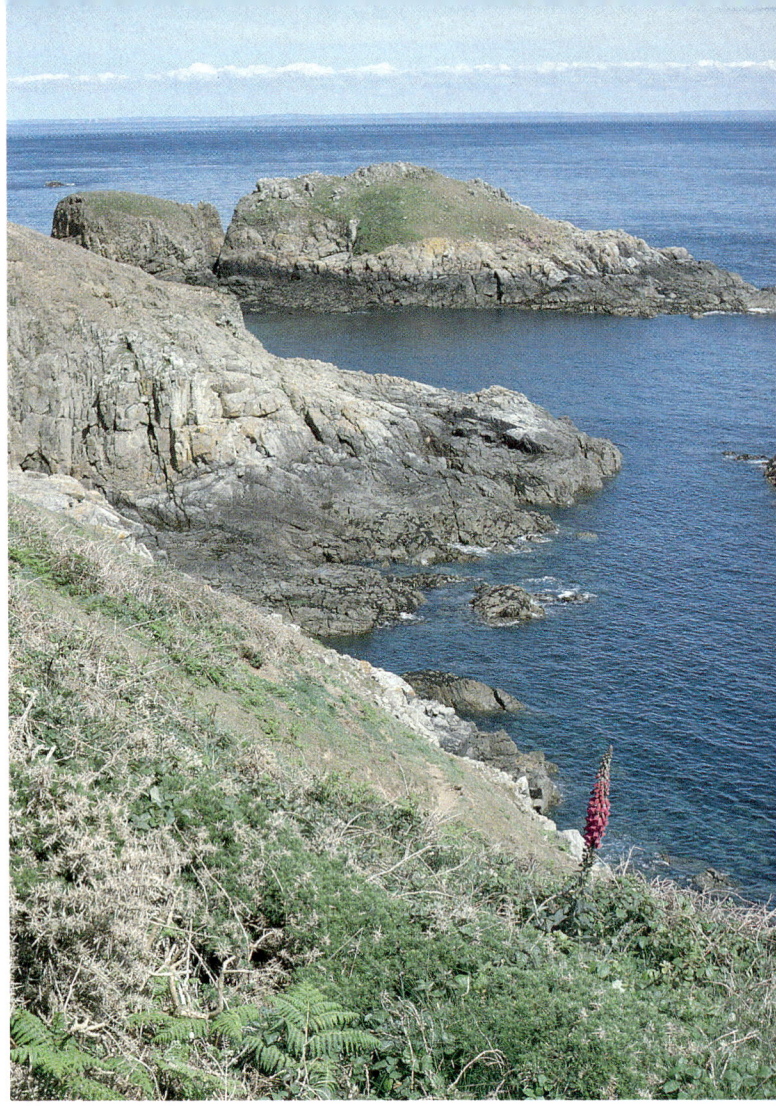

Little Sark. TOP LEFT: No. 44 On the way to Pot Bay there is this view of the east coast with Dixcart Bay visible in the background.

TOP RIGHT: No. 45 Looking across Clouet Bay towards Moie de la Brenière. This islet is separated from the main island by a narrow gully of water, except at low tide.

LEFT: No. 46 Reflections in Venus Pool. This circular tidal pool hidden beneath a cliff face in Clouet Bay was made famous by the artist William Toplis.

OPPOSITE TOP: No. 47 Steep-sided L'Etac lies quarter of a mile to the south of Little Sark and is 200 feet high. It is a haven for bird and plant life.

OPPOSITE BOTTOM: No. 48 The path that leads to Port Gorey. Part of a building is a reminder of the unsuccessful silver mining venture that was carried out in this area during the early 1800's.

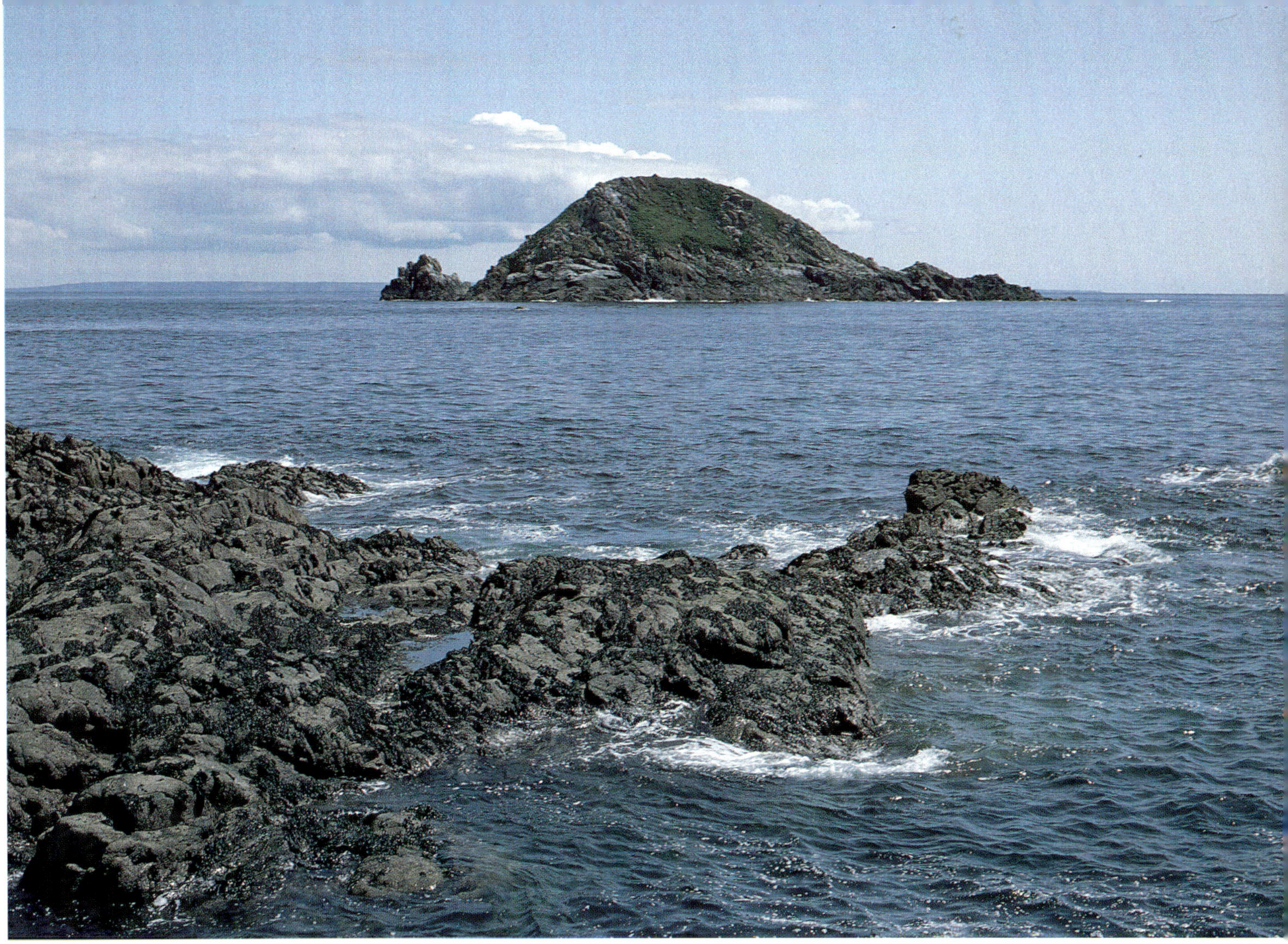

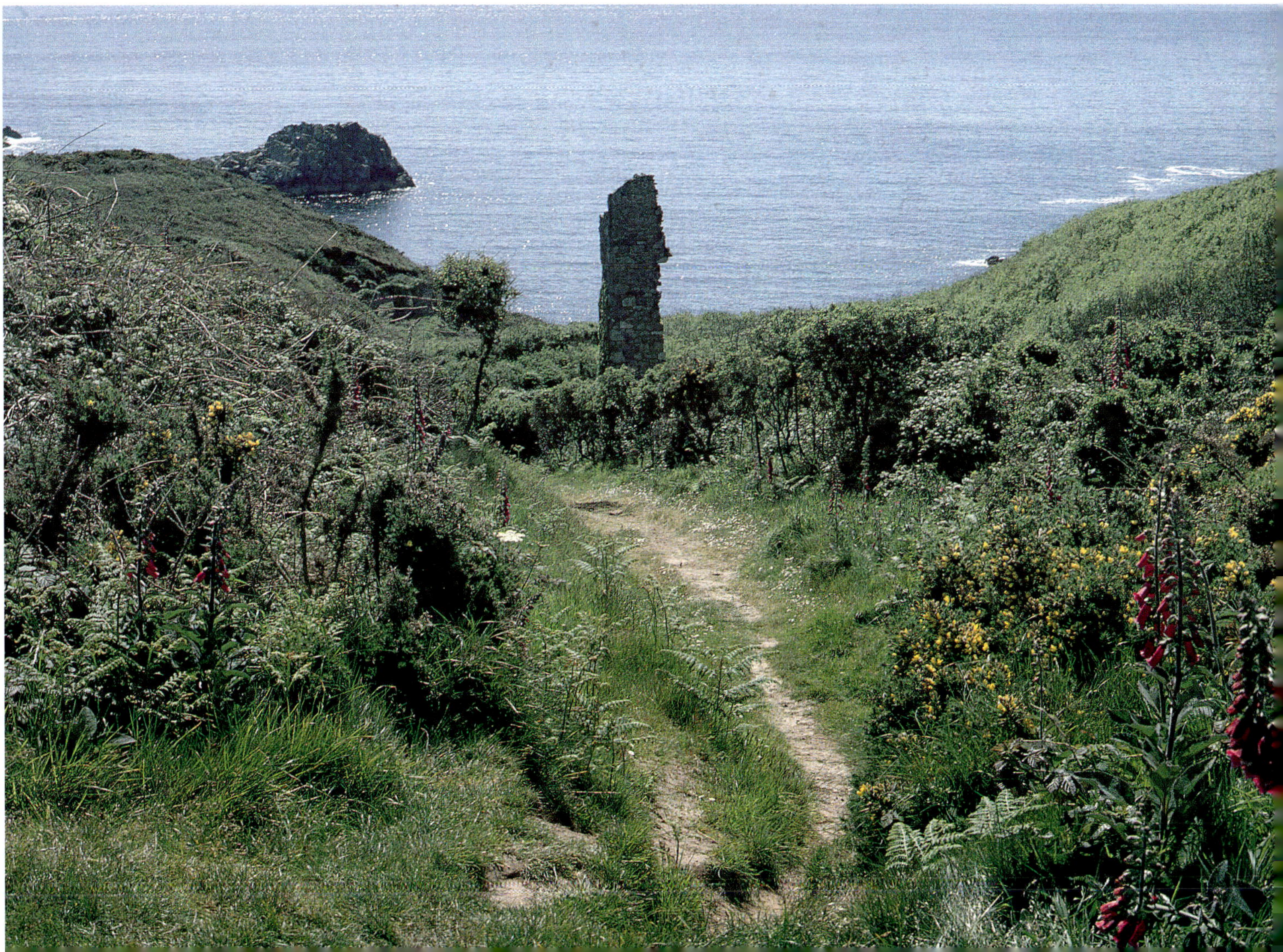

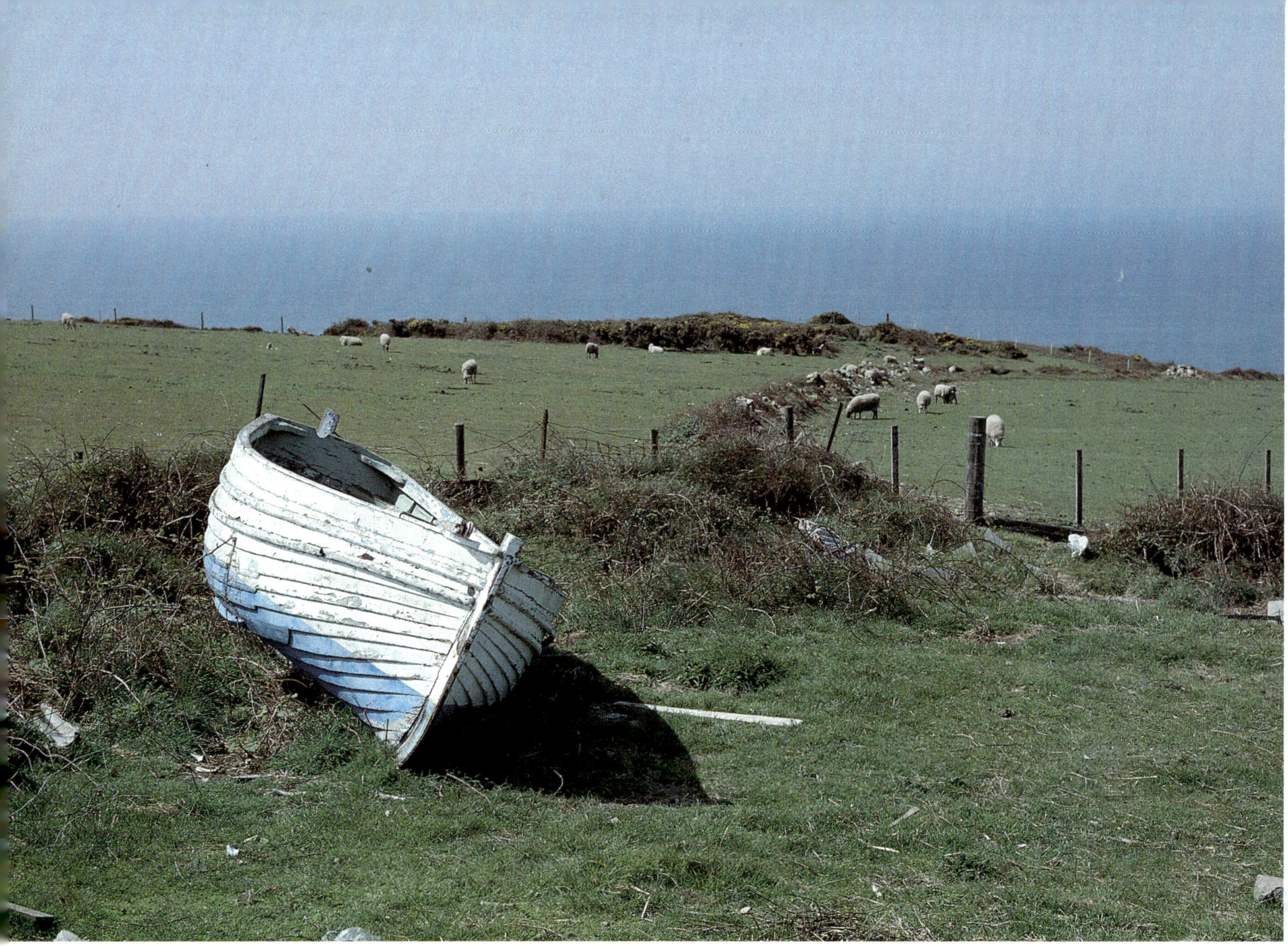

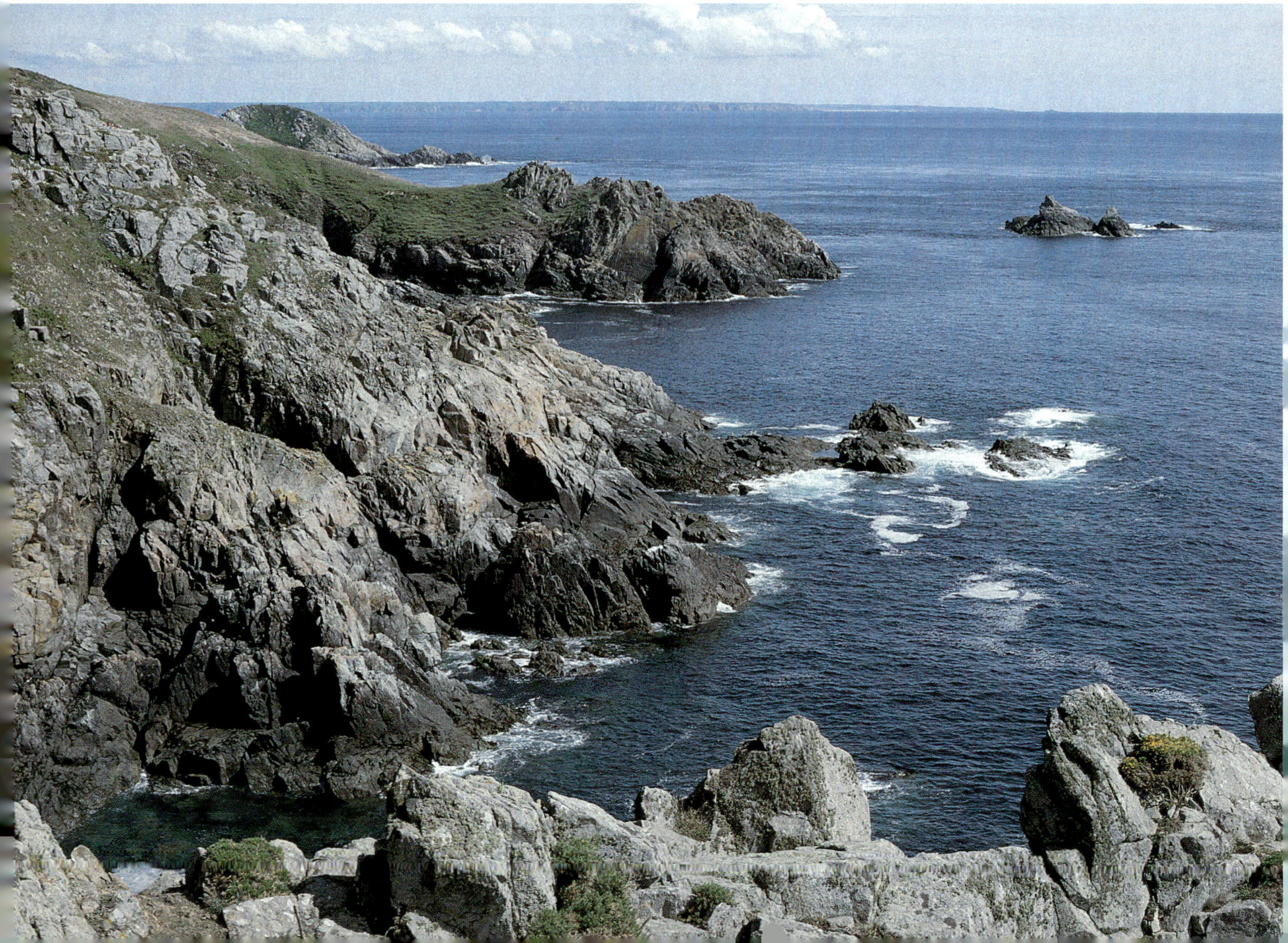

Little Sark. OPPOSITE TOP: No. 49 This boat lies in a field behind the Duval Farm.

OPPOSITE BOTTOM: No. 50 The rugged coastline of Rouge Câne Bay. At low tide a number of rock pools are exposed, including the Adonis which is the deepest and largest in Sark. Jersey can be seen in the background.

TOP: No. 51 Holiday-makers rest at the corner of La Sablonnerie Hotel.

RIGHT: No. 52 When in the Island don't forget a Sark cream tea!

LEFT: No. 53 What is there to do on a foggy Good Friday morning? Why not join the spectators at the Beauregard Duckpond.

BELOW: No. 54 There you can watch the traditional sailing of the model yachts, some of which are very old.

OPPOSITE TOP: No. 55 An old granite cider press in its last resting place outside La Moinerie Hotel.

OPPOSITE BOTTOM: No. 56 Carriages parked outside the Seigneurie gate while the passengers enjoy a visit to the beautiful walled garden.

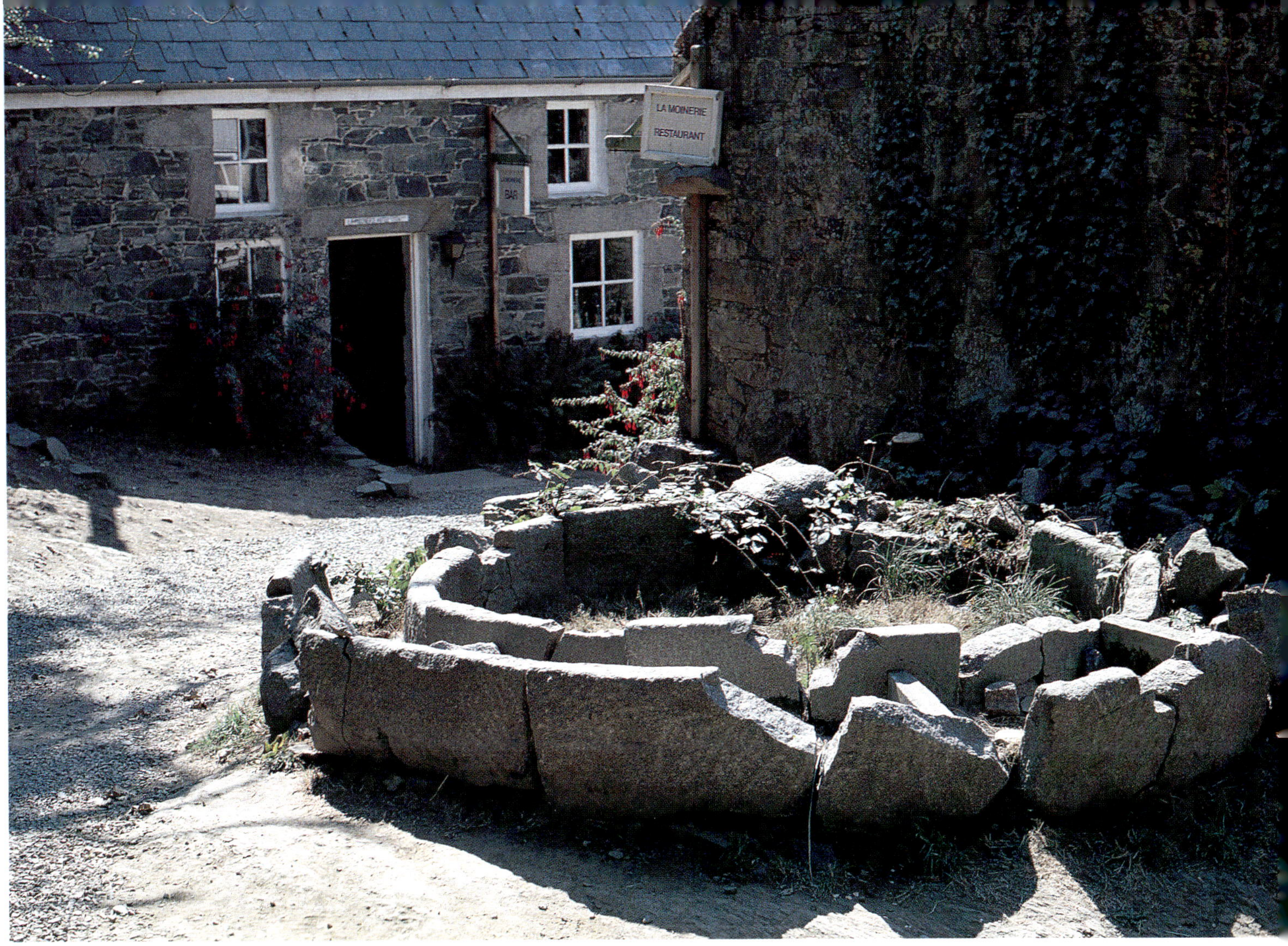
LA MOINERIE
RESTAURANT
BAR

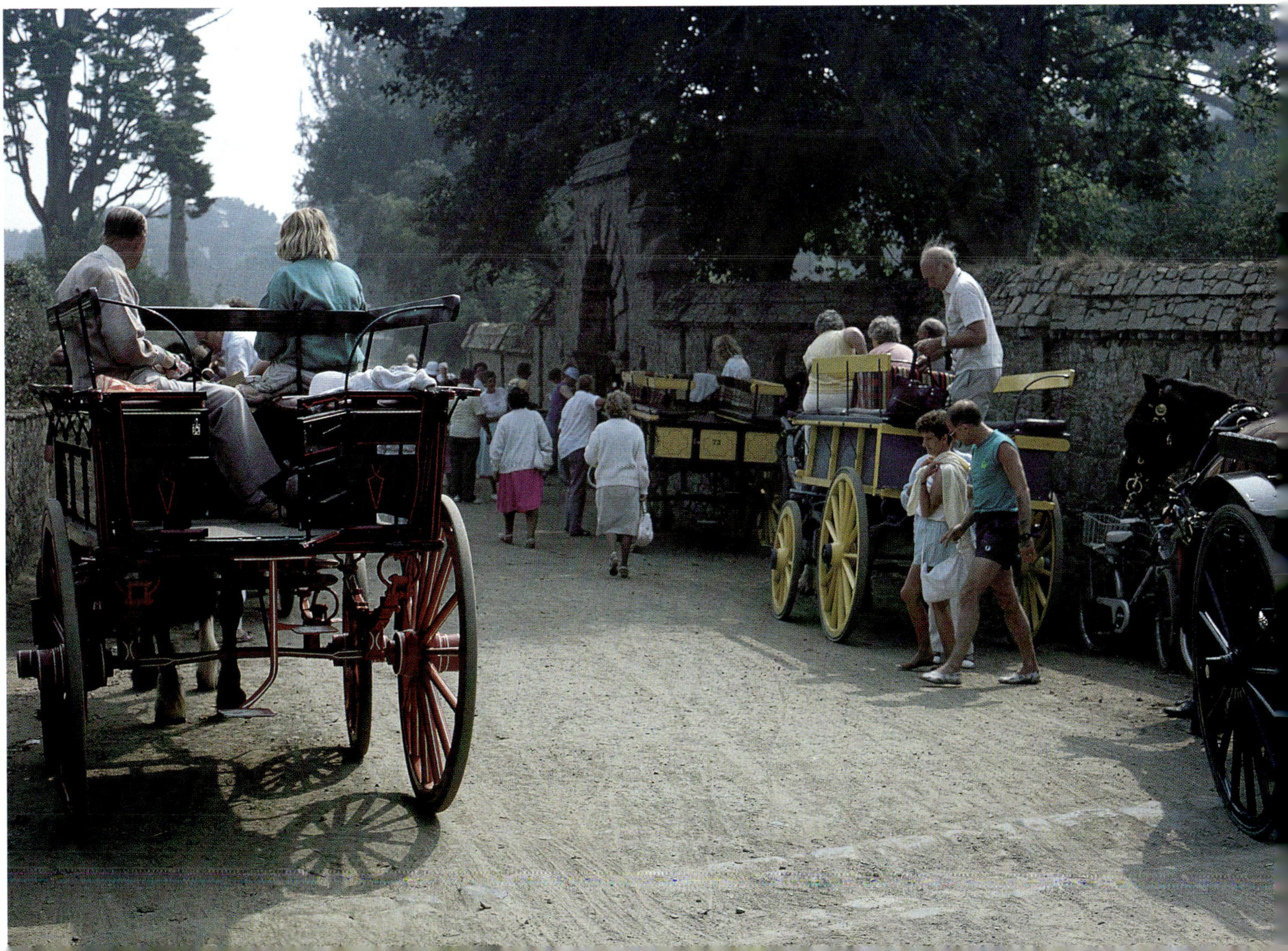

La Seigneurie. TOP: No. 57 Roses flourish in the garden sheltered by high walls and trees.

LEFT: No. 58 A close-up of the Seigneurie front door. Carved in the lintel is the actual longitude and latitude of the house.

OPPOSITE TOP: No. 59 The Seigneurie as seen from the walled garden. The house became the Seigneurie in 1730 and the tower was added later in 1860 by the Reverend W.T.Collings, the Seigneur at that time.

OPPOSITE BOTTOM LEFT: No. 60 Bright flowers decorate the archways in the garden wall.

OPPOSITE BOTTOM RIGHT: No. 61 This brass cannon is inscribed with the date 1572 and was presented by Queen Elizabeth I to Helier de Carteret, the first Seigneur of the Island.

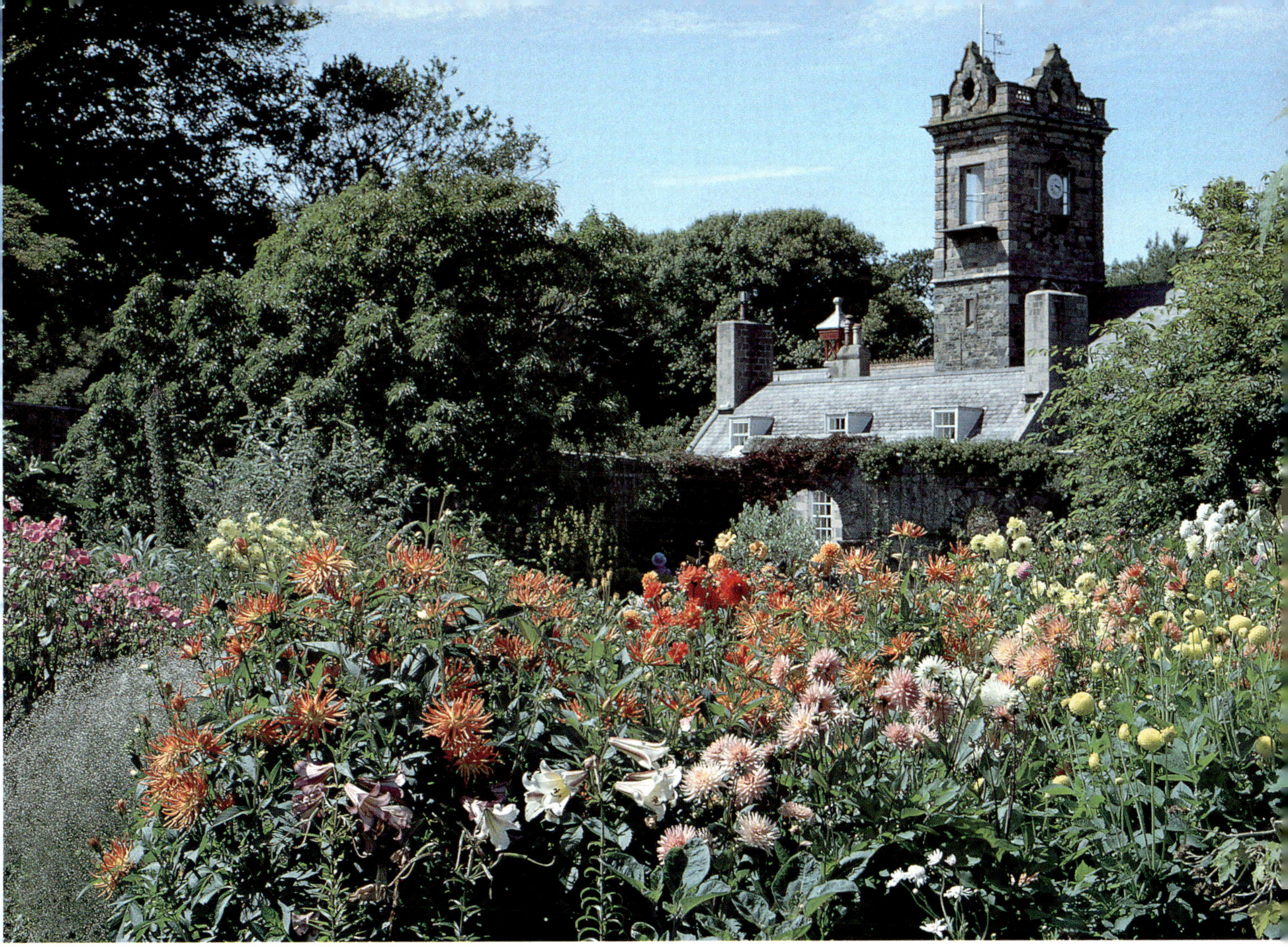
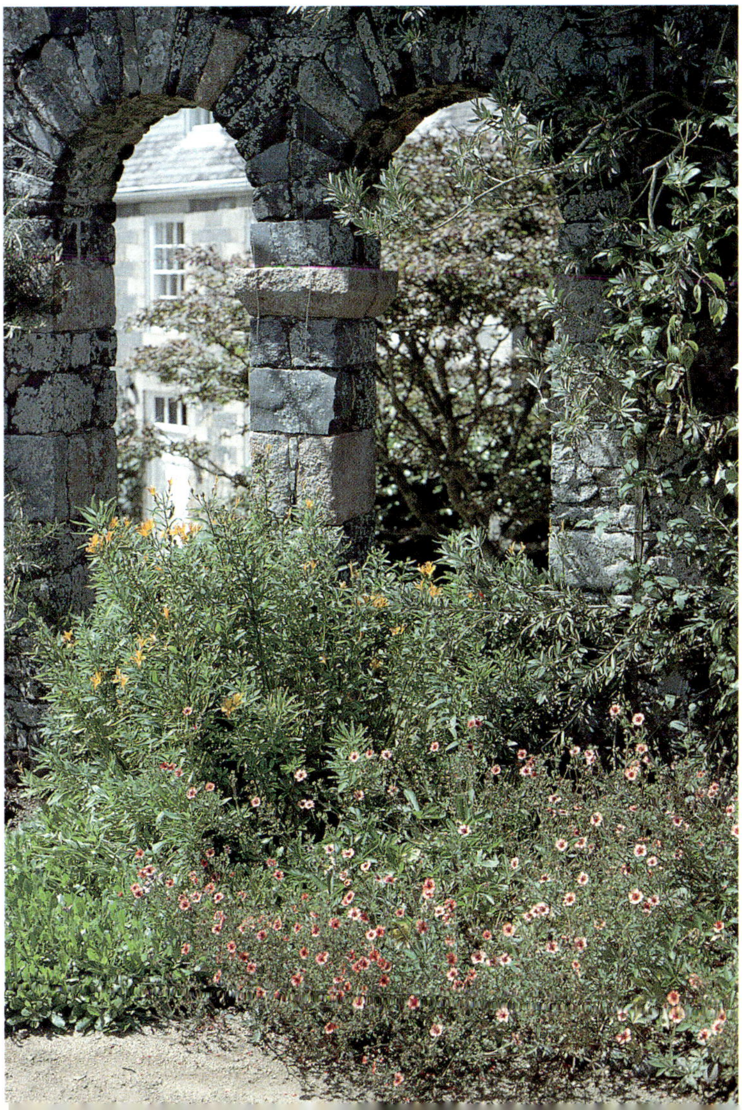
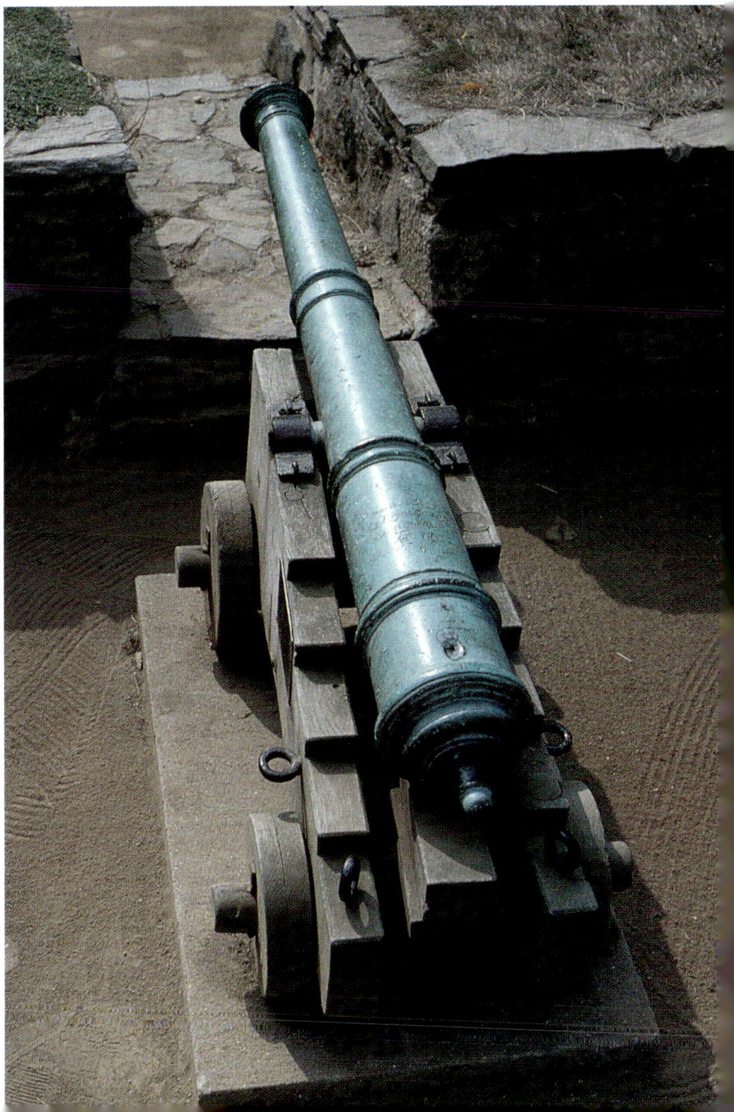

ABOVE: No. 62 Looking from Havre Gosselin towards Grande Grève with its flotilla of little boats.

OPPOSITE TOP LEFT: No. 63 A small vessel approaches the Gouliot Passage renowed for its swift tidal run. The channel separates the Island of Brecqhou from the main Island of Sark.

OPPOSITE TOP RIGHT: No. 64 Making their way up the cliff from the Havre Gosselin and its sheltered anchorage from east winds. Herm is just visible in the background.

OPPOSITE BOTTOM: No. 65 A local fisherman sets out with his boat piled up with pots hoping for a good catch of lobsters and crabs. The dark shadows in the cliff hide openings to the Gouliot Caves.

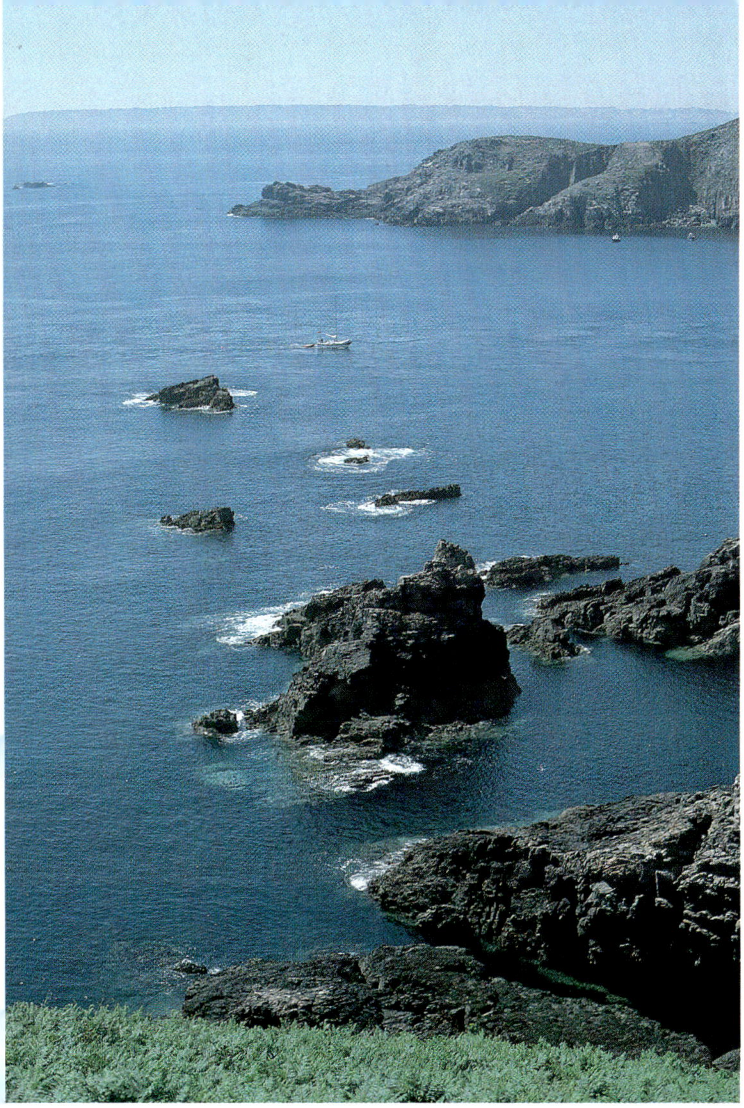
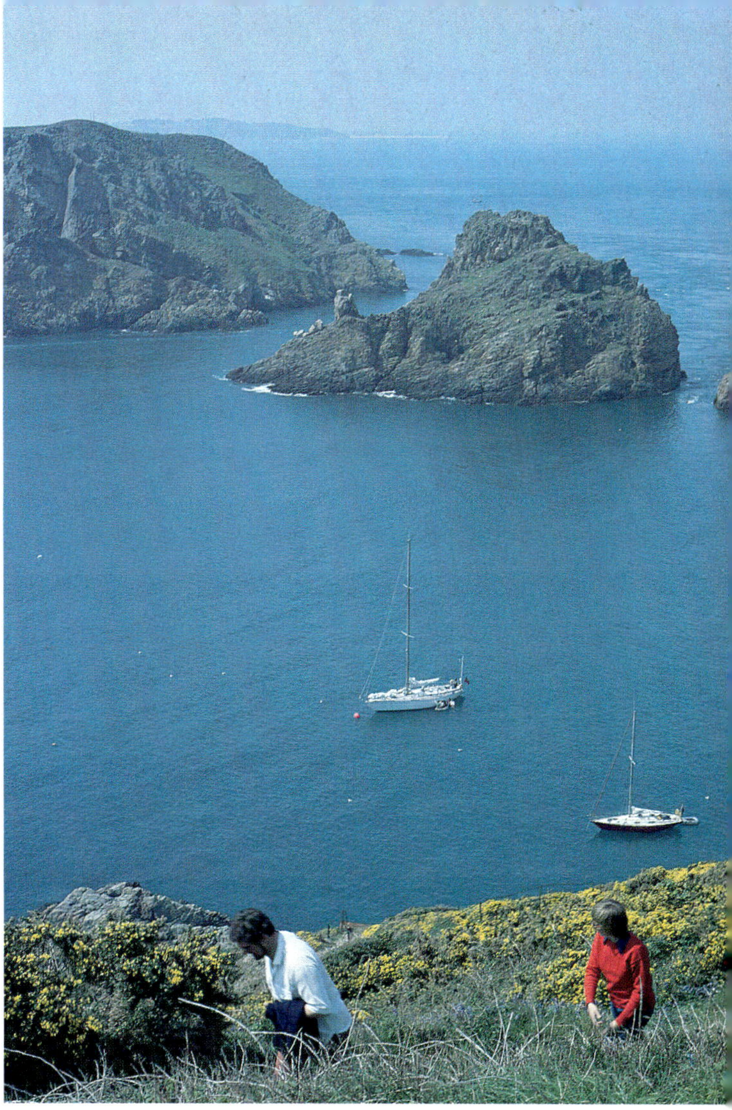
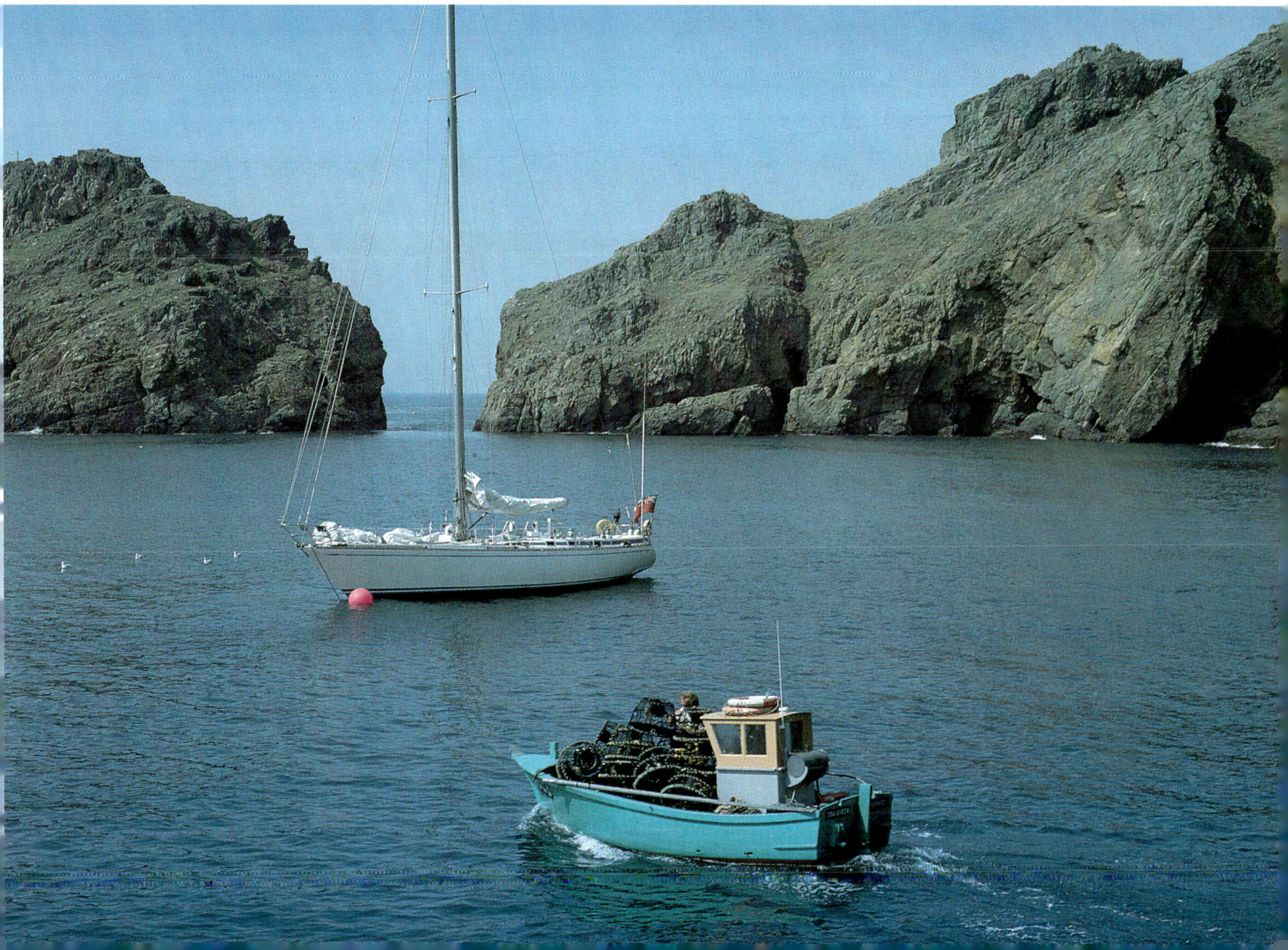

ABOVE: No. 66 Sark has many interesting tunnels and caves. This sea entrance is in Derrible Bay and is one of the ways that lead to Creux Derrible.

OPPOSITE TOP: No. 67 Green and red anemones caught by flashlight in the Jewel Cave which is part of the Gouliot Caves complex.

OPPOSITE BOTTOM. No. 68 Sunlight reflects on a pool at the entrance to one of the sea openings of the Gouliot Caves.

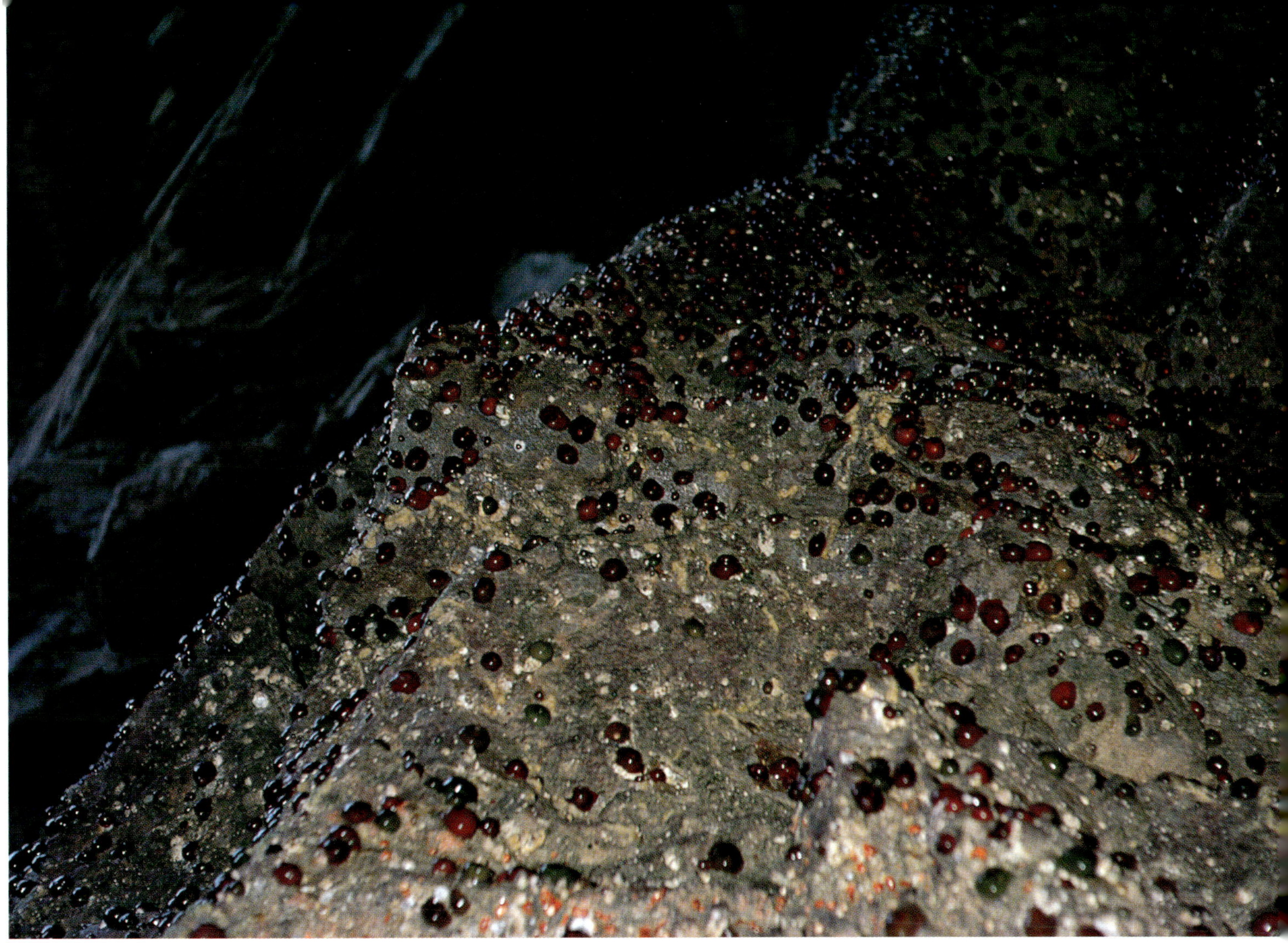

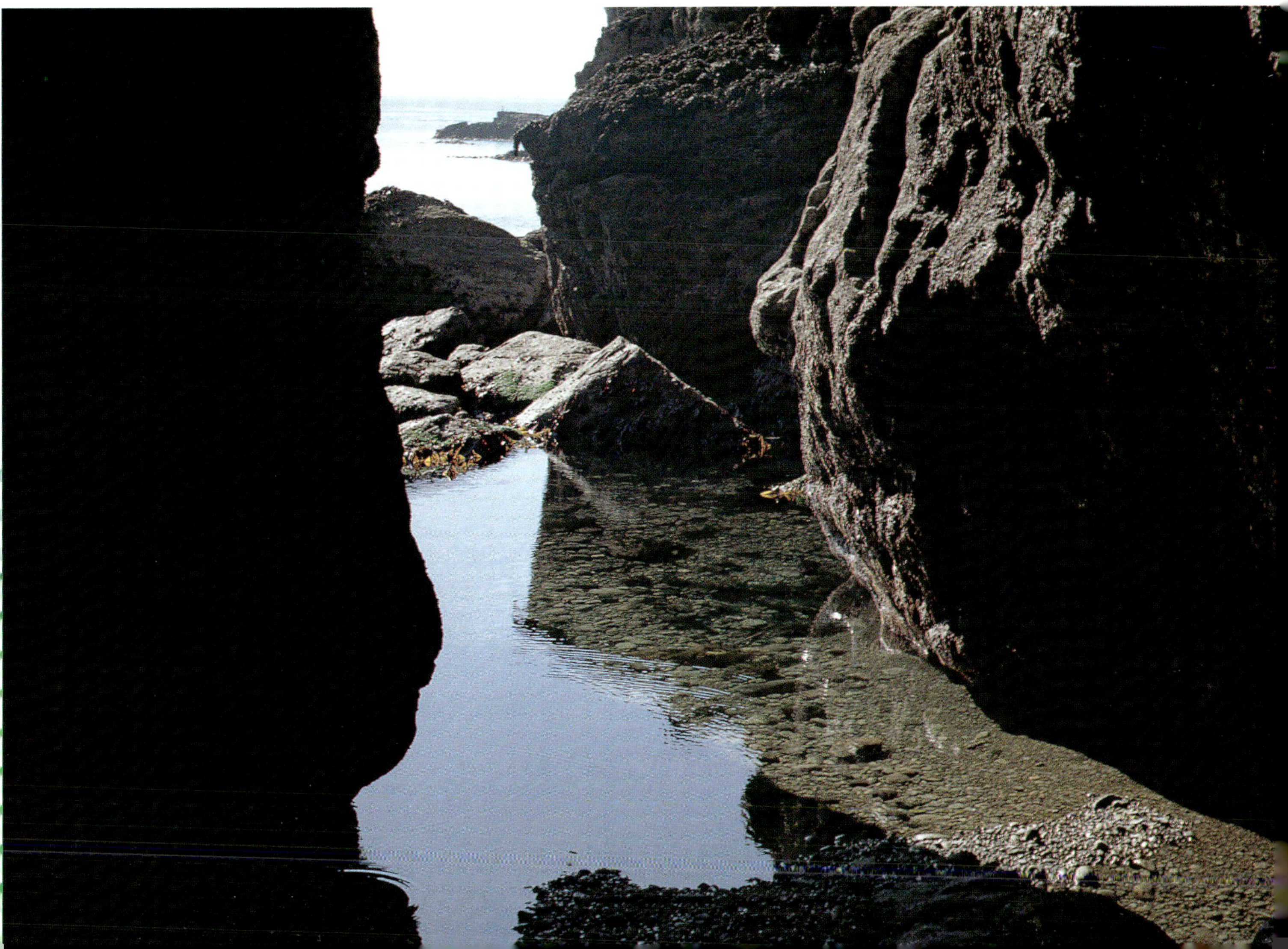

ABOVE: No. 69 Le Vieux Port, an old farm of great character is on the path that leads to Port à la Jument Bay.

LEFT: No. 70 A contented cat enjoys a snooze on top of a wall above the farm.

OPPOSITE TOP: No. 71 A carriage passes by the side of Le Port à la Jument showing part of the beautiful garden.

OPPOSITE BOTTOM: No. 72 Port à la Jument Bay. This bay is only accessible from half tide when, as the water recedes, a fine expanse of sand is revealed.

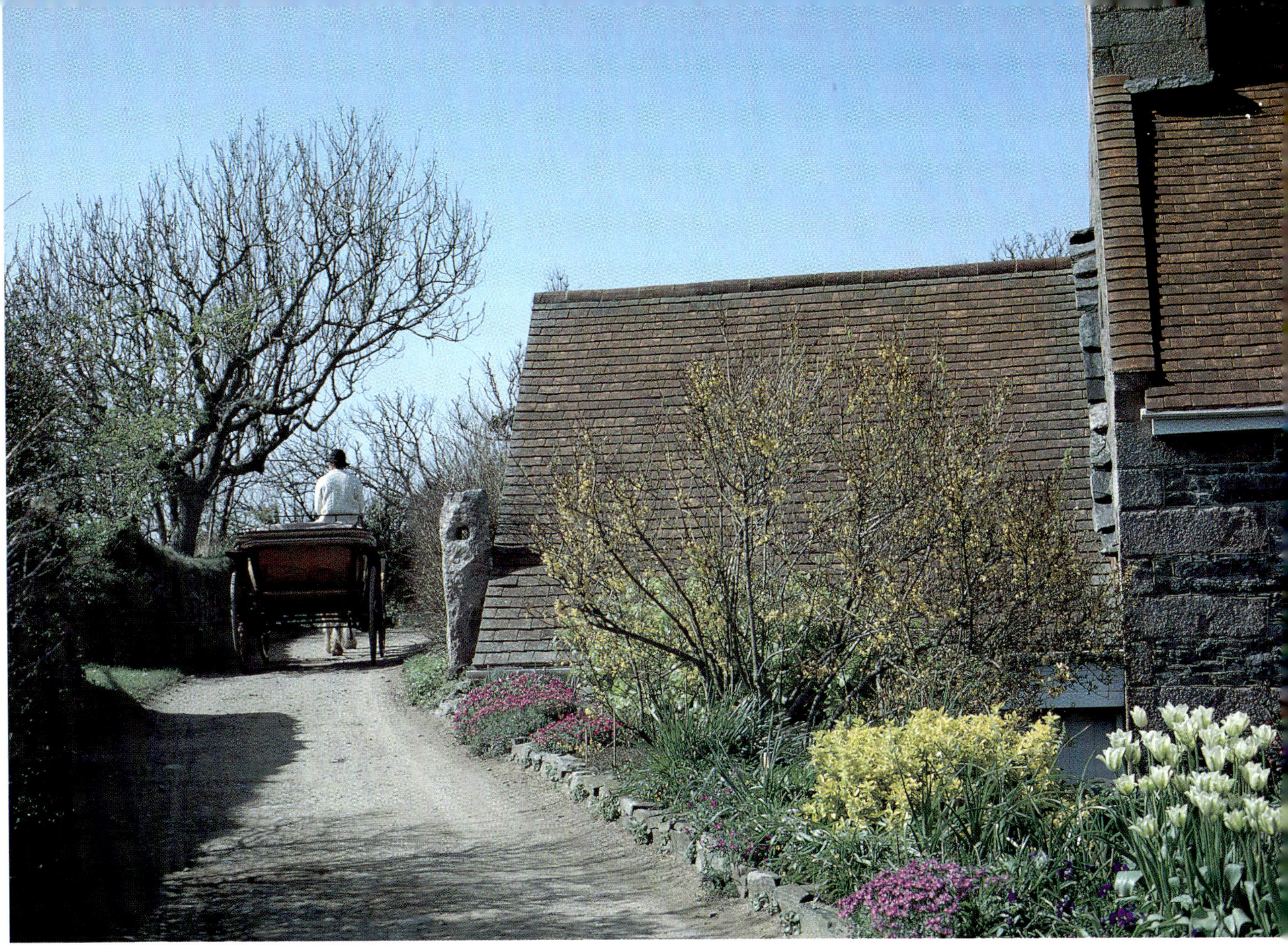

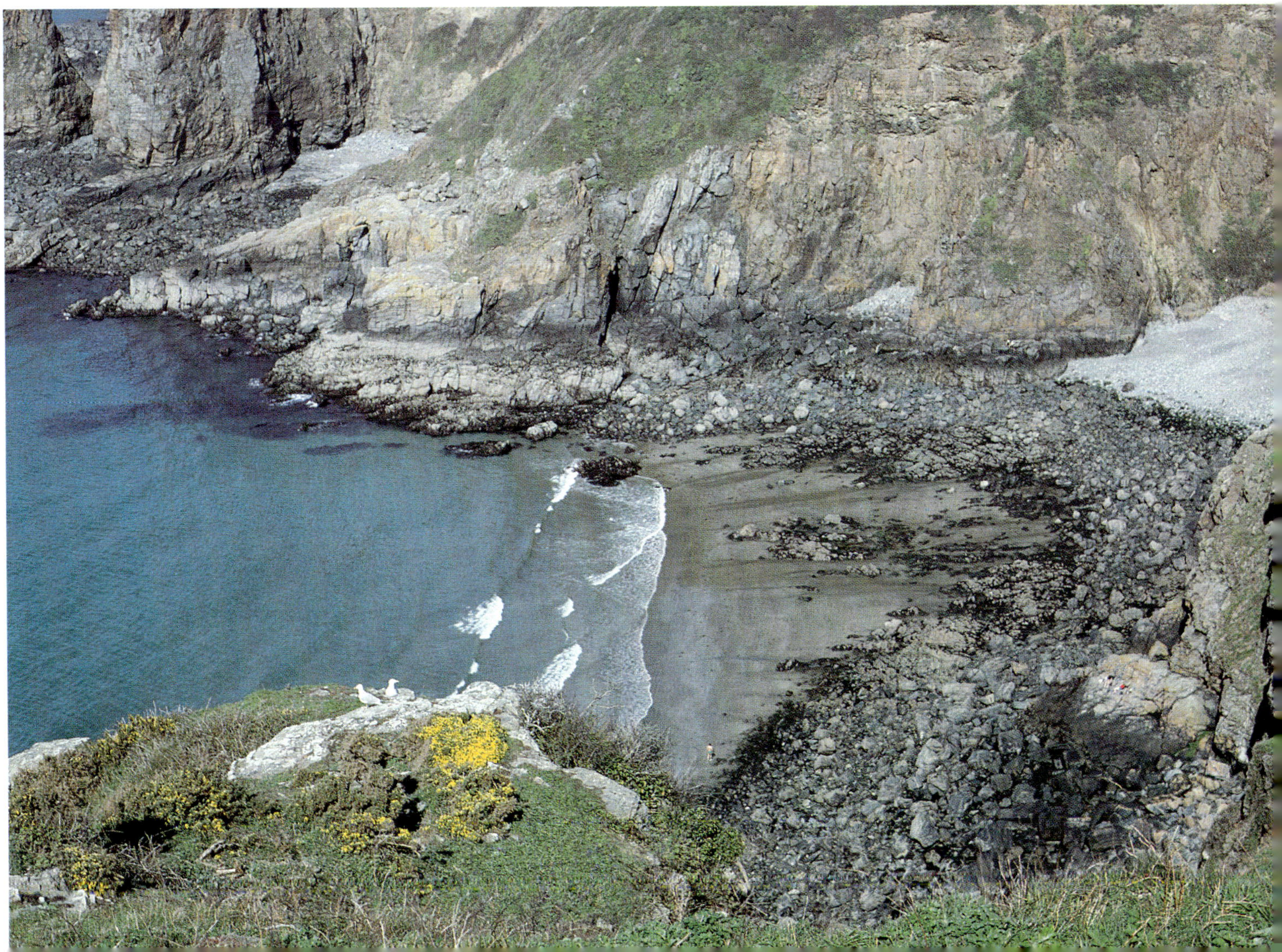

ABOVE: No. 73 Looking across Pégâne Bay towards the rock mass of Tintageu. Beyond this the coast leads away towards the northern tip of the Island.

LEFT: No. 74 Port du Moulin Bay in the foreground with Les Autelets beyond. These impressive rock stacks can be reached at low tide and are popular with ornithologists and artists alike.

OPPOSITE: No. 75 The magnificent arch at the northern edge of Port du Moulin. One of the Autelets can just be seen through the gap.

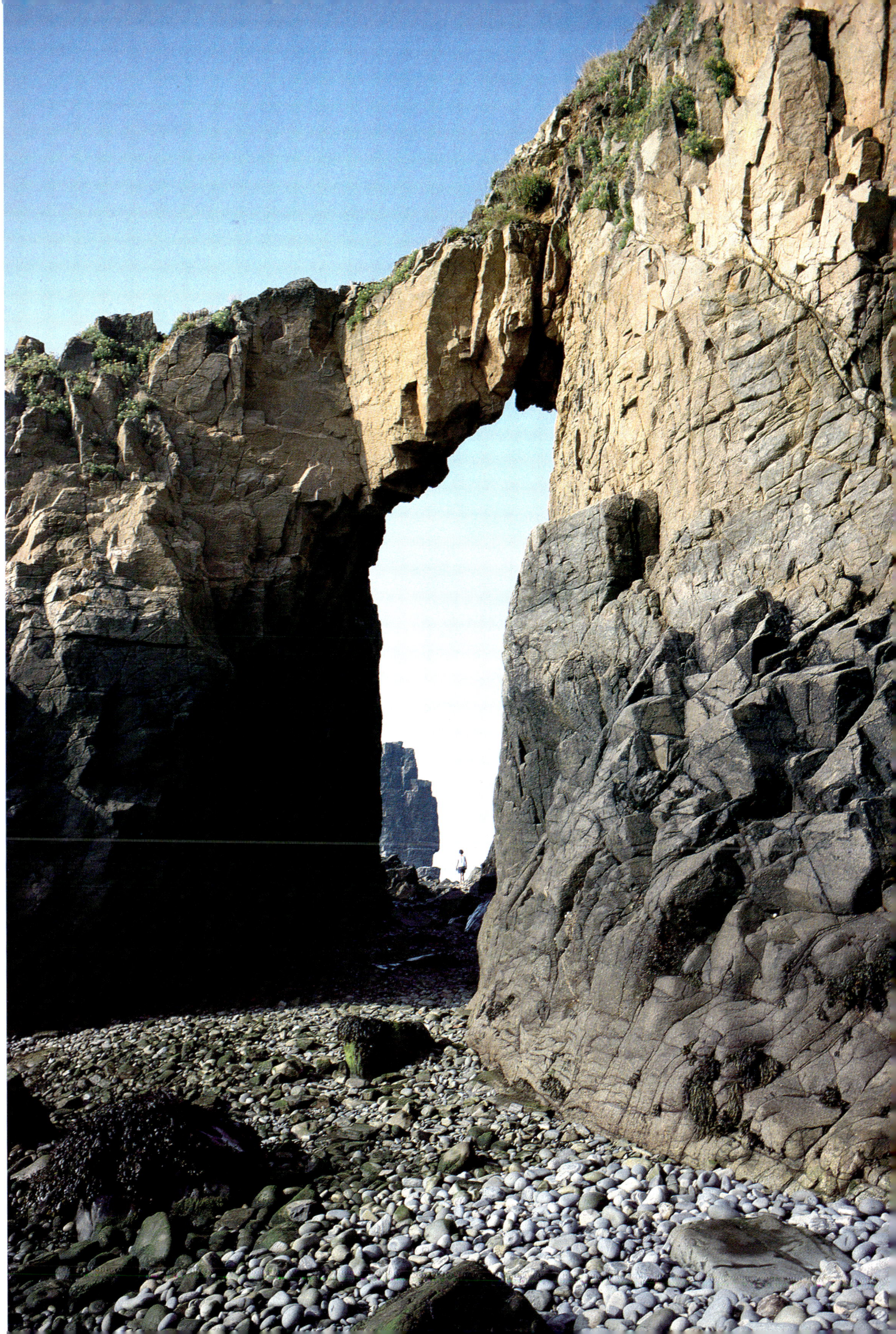

Some aspects of Sark life. LEFT: No. 76 Children's cycles await their owners against the wall of the Junior School.

BOTTOM: No. 77 More cycles against the corner of an old house near the Island Prison.

OPPOSITE TOP: No. 78 Certainly free range here on this track in Little Sark.

OPPOSITE BOTTOM LEFT: No. 79 An old spade rests against a farm wall.

OPPOSITE BOTTOM RIGHT: No. 80 A thick vein of quartz running through the rock near the Venus Pool.

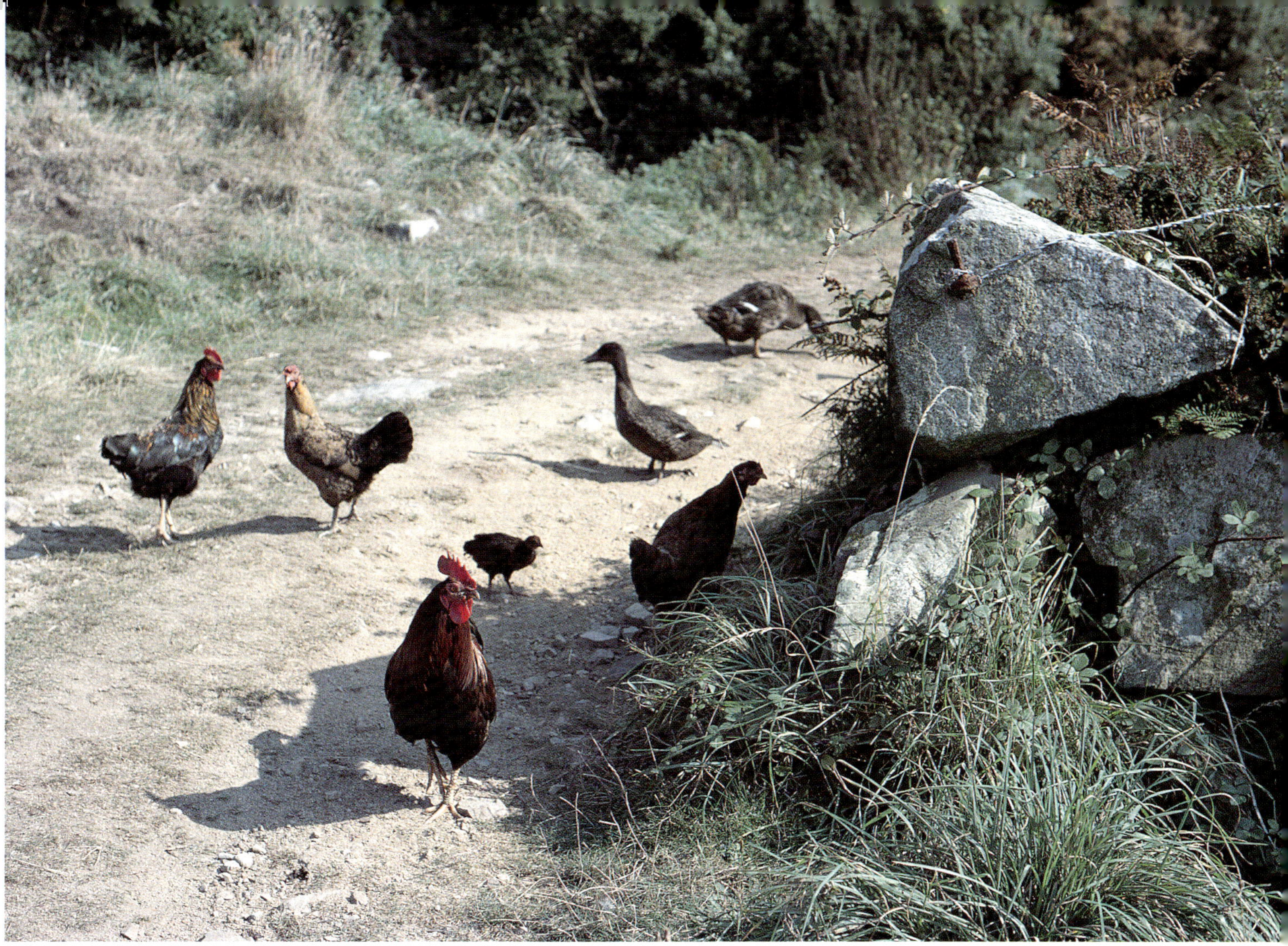

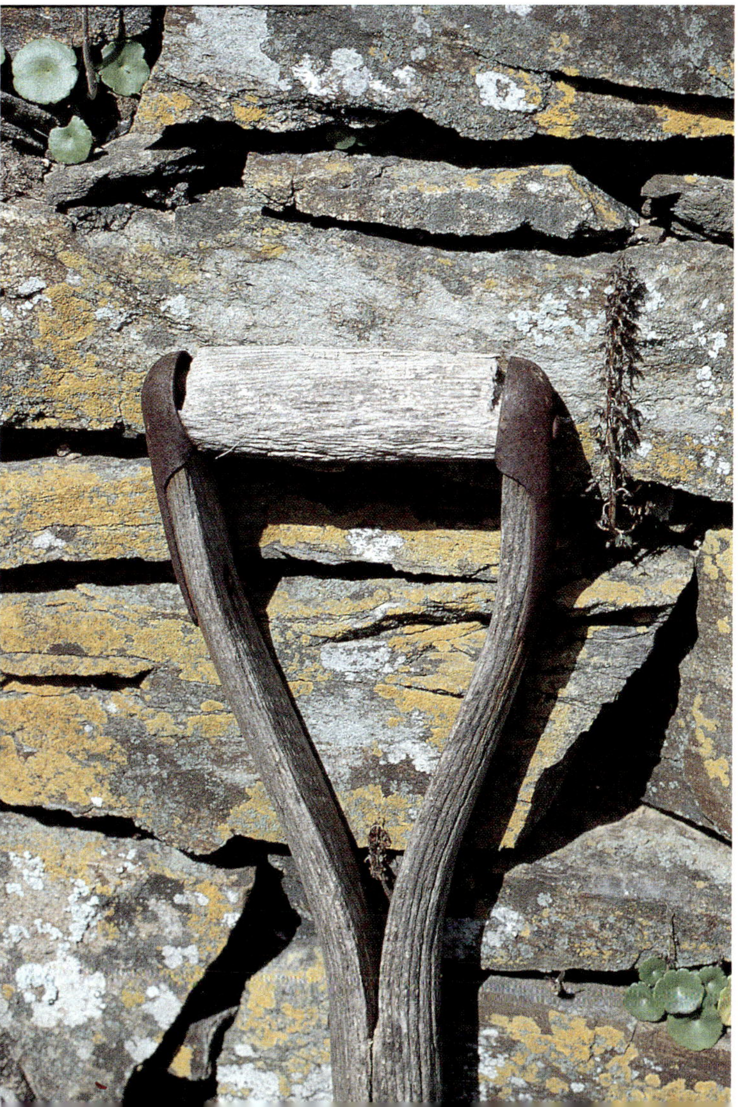

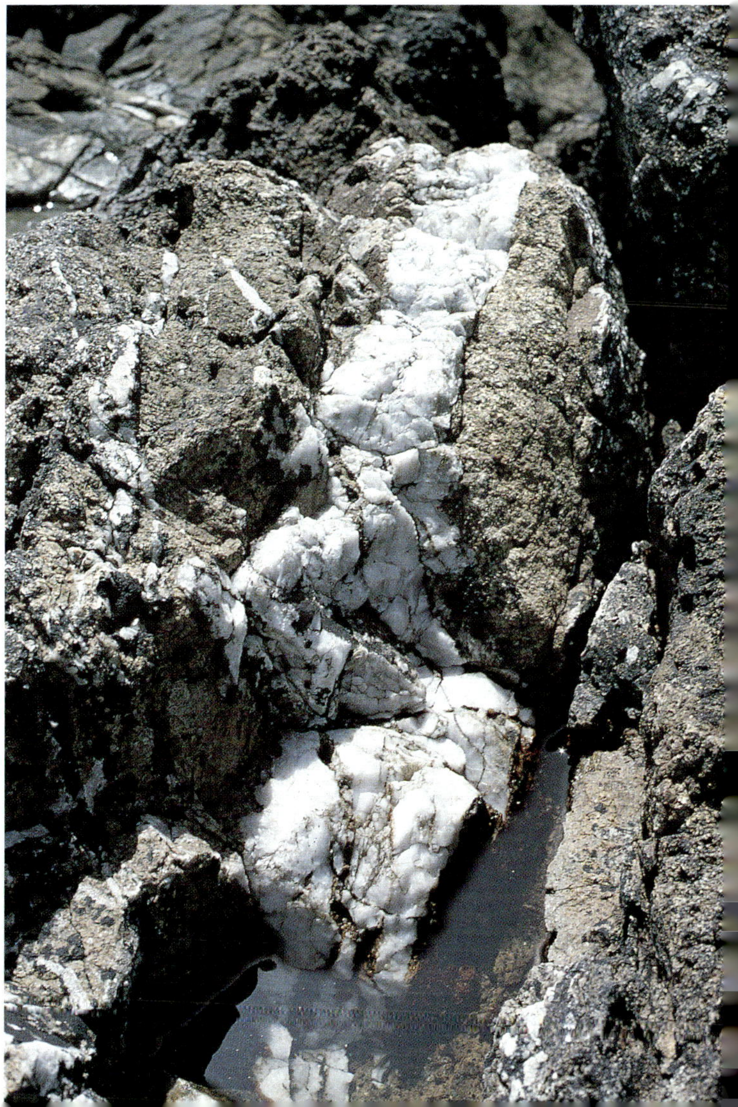

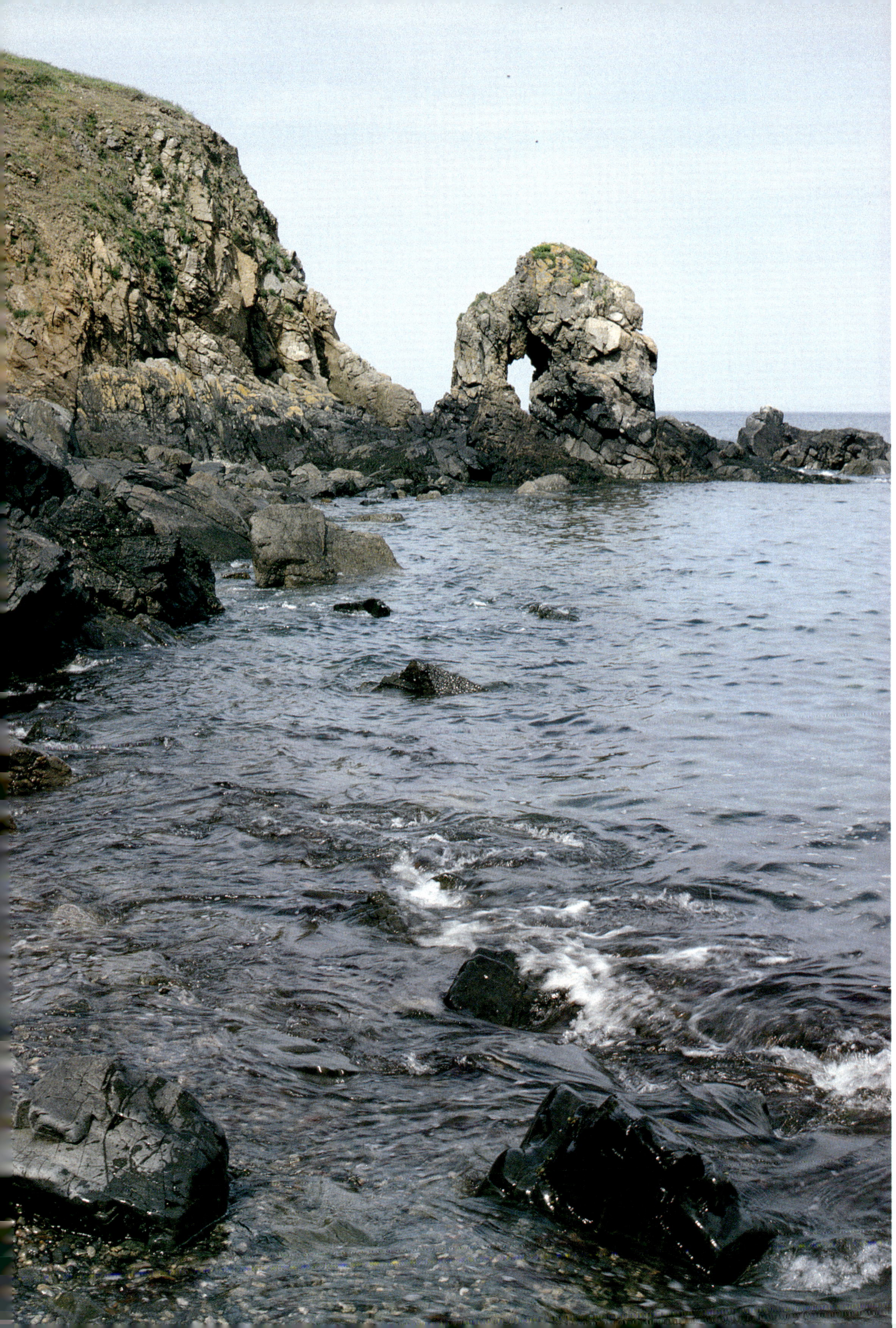

OPPOSITE: No. 81 Below the Eperquerie Common on the east coast is Les Fontaines Bay. At its northern edge is the Fairy Grotto consisting of two arches, one behind the other.

RIGHT: No. 82 Looking south from Les Fontaines towards Grande Creux. An area with a number of caves to explore at suitable tides.

BOTTOM: No. 83 An impressive striped boulder. Pottering around the beaches can be very rewarding especially on a wet day when the dampness brings out the colours in the stones.

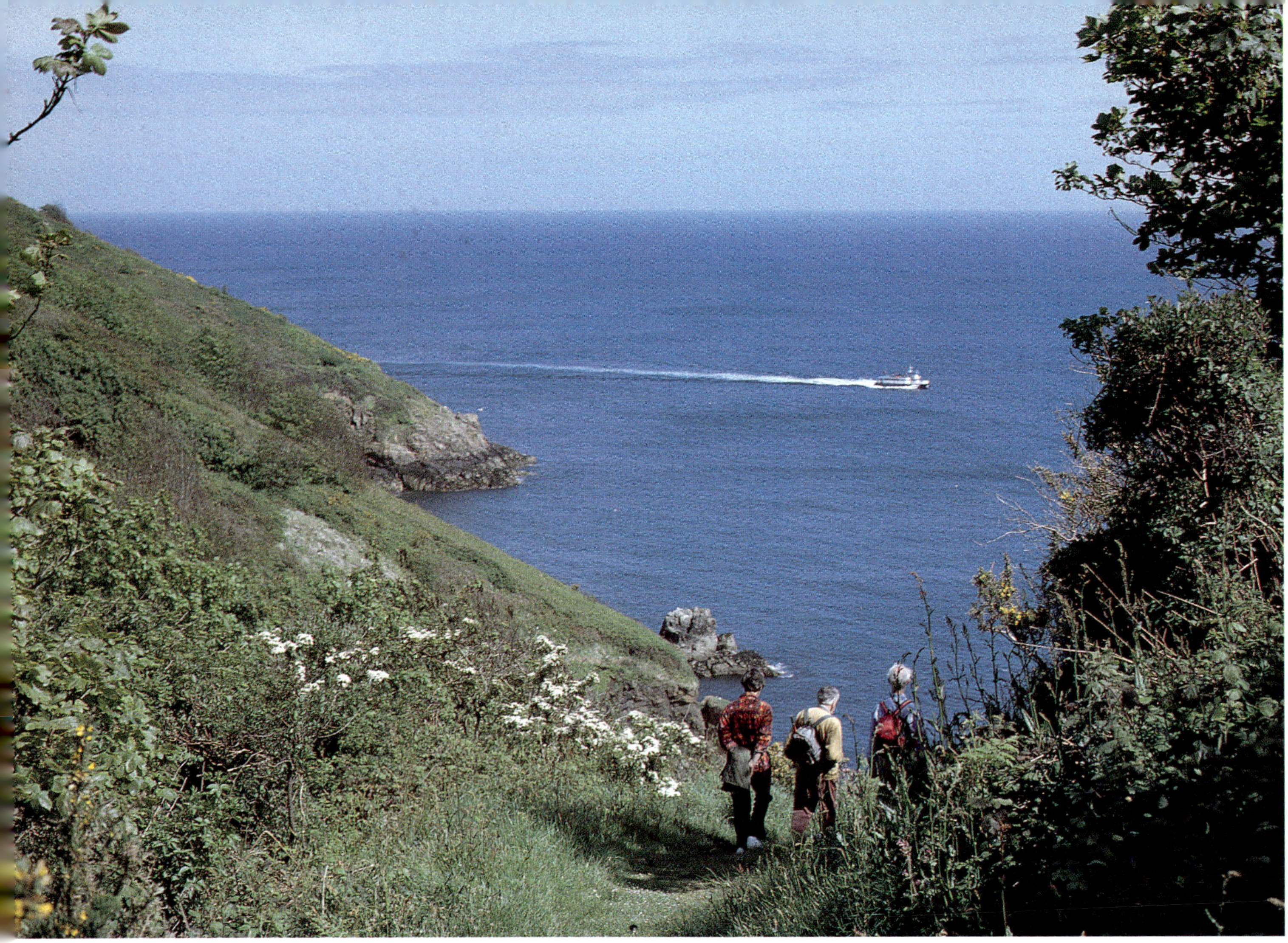

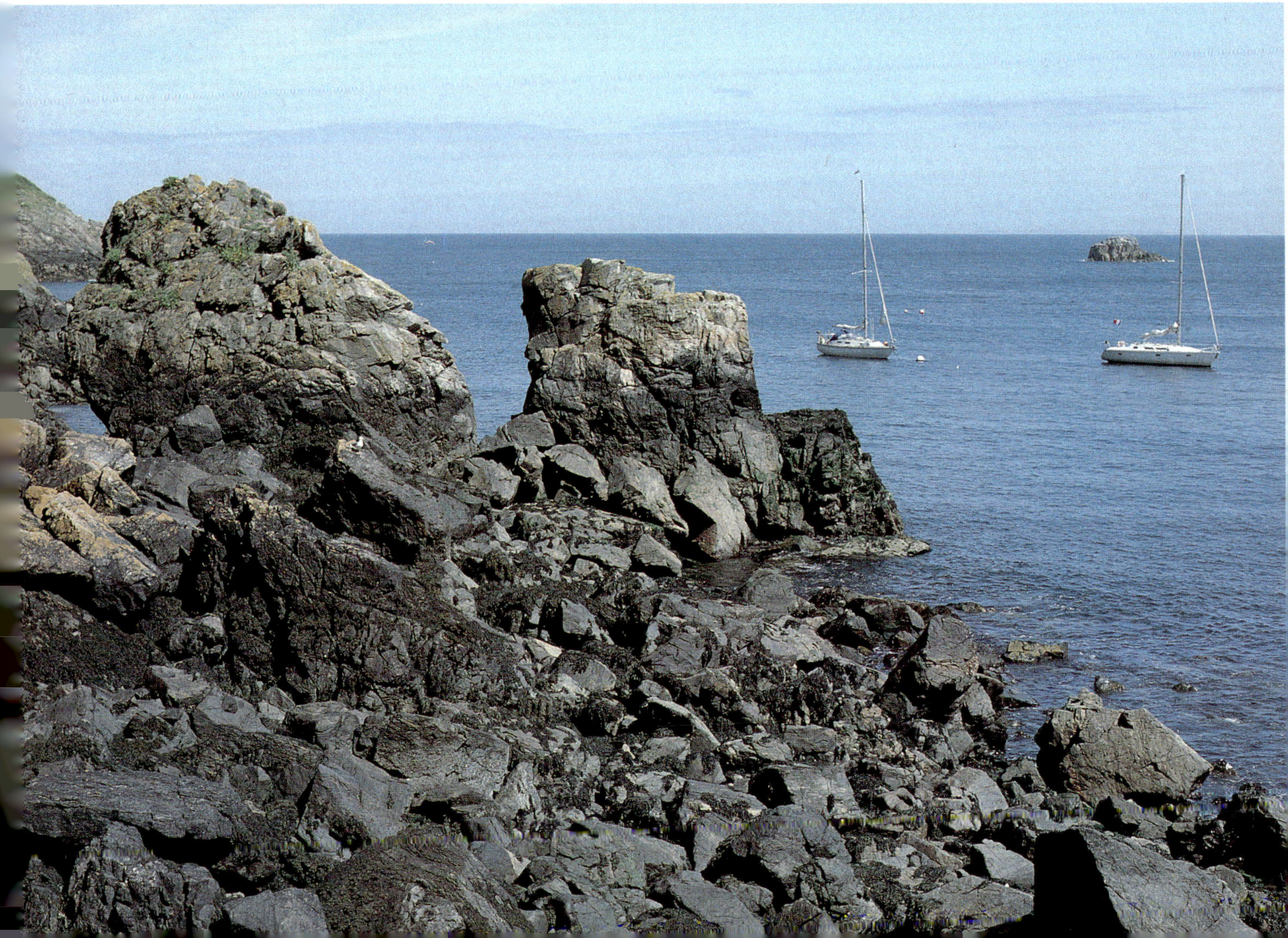

Grève de la Ville. OPPOSITE TOP: No. 84 On the path that descends to the bay. Out to sea a passenger boat makes its way towards the Maseline Harbour.

OPPOSITE BOTTOM: No. 85 Visiting yachts moored to the north of the bay.

RIGHT: No. 86 Beneath the headland at the southern edge of the bay is the Gulls Chapel.

BOTTOM: No. 87 Looking through the Gulls Chapel into the bay. Grève de la Ville faces north - east and is a good place to visit in the morning.

A last look around.
TOP: No. 89 A flock of sheep in a field above Dixcart valley.

LEFT: No. 90 A horse grazes in a field to the south of La Seigneurie.

OPPOSITE: No. 91 Impressive rock strata at Tintageu at the southern edge of Port du Moulin.

THE ISLAND OF SARK

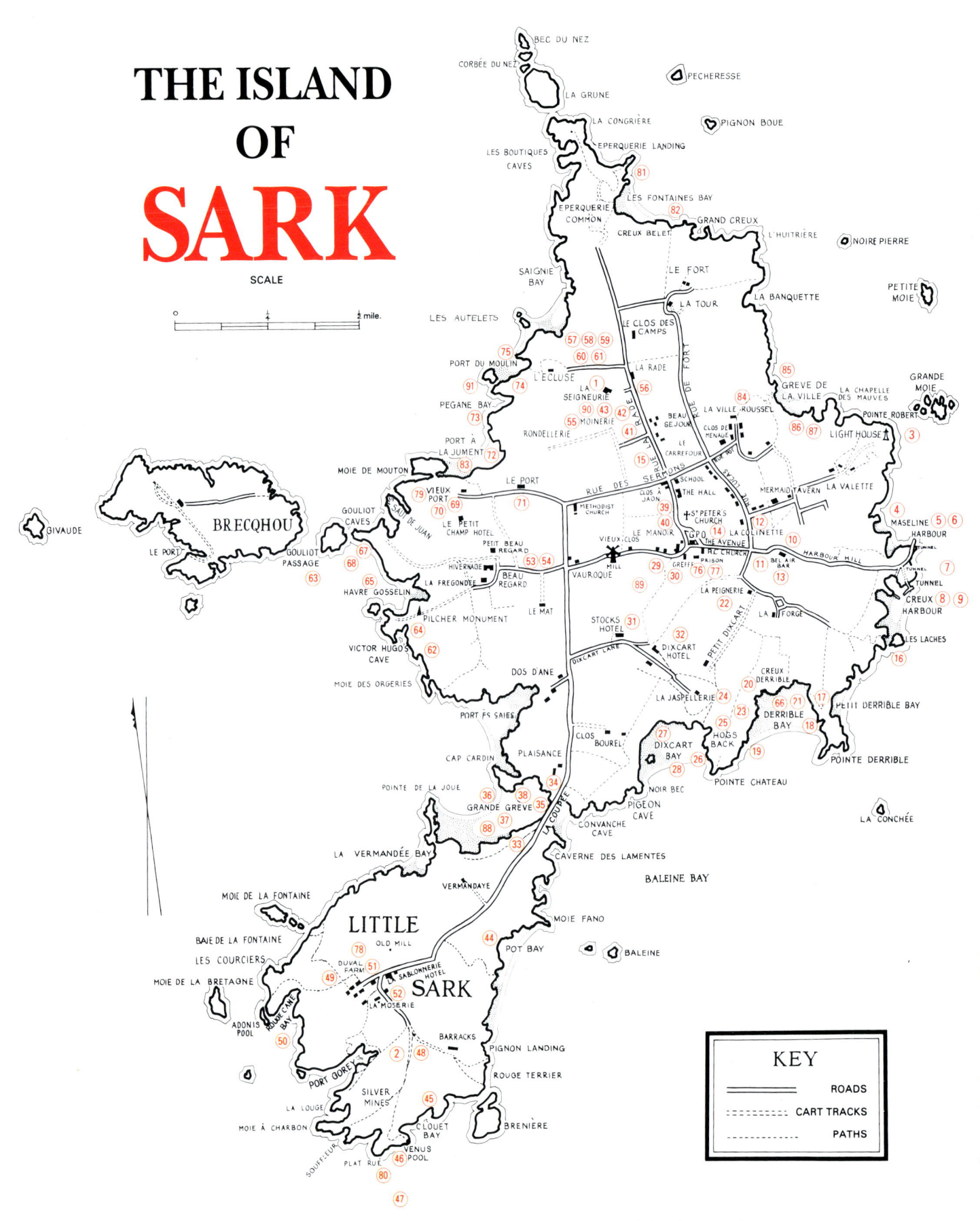

SCALE
0 — ¼ — ½ mile

KEY
— ROADS
⋯⋯ CART TRACKS
- - - PATHS

The numbers on the map show the approximate location of the photographs